THE
60
SECOND
ORGANIZER

Sixty Solid Techniques
for Beating Chaos
at Home and at Work

JEFF DAVIDSON

ADAMS MEDIA
Avon, Massachusetts

Published by
Adams Media, an F+W Publications Company
57 Littlefield Street, Avon, MA 02322. U.S.A.
www.adamsmedia.com

ISBN: 1-59337-105-5

Printed in Canada.

J I H G F E D C

Library of Congress Cataloging-in-Publication Data

Davidson, Jeffrey P.
The 60 second organizer / by Jeff Davidson.
p.   cm.
ISBN 1-59337-105-5
1. Time management. I. Title: Sixty second organizer. II. Title.

BF637.T5D38 2004
640'.43—dc22

2004005865

This publication is designed to provide accurate and authoritative information with regard to the subject matter covered. It is sold with the understanding that the publisher is not engaged in rendering legal, accounting, or other professional advice. If legal advice or other expert assistance is required, the services of a competent professional person should be sought.
—From a *Declaration of Principles* jointly adopted by a Committee of the American Bar Association and a Committee of Publishers and Associations

Many of the designations used by manufacturers and sellers to distinguish their products are claimed as trademarks. Where those designations appear in this book and Adams Media was aware of a trademark claim, the designations have been printed with initial capital letters.

This book is available at quantity discounts for bulk purchases.
For information, call 1-800-872-5627.

Contents

Part One: Embracing Powerful Perspectives

Part Two: Enveloping Provocative Practices

Part Three: Listing and Charting Your Way

Part Four: Reclaiming Your Places and Spaces

Part Five: Organize Travel, Meetings, and Online Activities

Part Six: Making Your Home Your Castle

Foreword

SOMETIMES, WHEN I AM TRYING TO CONCENTRATE on a project, out of the corner of my eye, I notice something on my desk related to another project. I start dwelling on this other task and I get distracted from my work. As Jeff Davidson will explain, it is not the other task that creates the delay, but the meandering and lack of focus that steers me away. Lack of organization costs me time and mental energy.

Reading *The 60 Second Organizer* reorganized my mind in preparation for cleaning up my desk. The time I spent reading Jeff's advice prepared my mind for reorganizing in the same way that stretching prepares my body for tennis. This is the way Jeff approaches organizing—as an exercise in control, efficiency, and peace of mind.

When you read *The 60 Second Organizer*, you'll learn how each of the 60 tips—one for each second in the minute—can help you restore order to any area of your life whether, it be your desk, car, or kitchen table. If one tip can't get you moving, you can easily and quickly flip to one that will. In seconds, you'll pick up a nugget or two and find yourself on the path to reclaiming your life.

Now that my debris is cleared away, I'm beginning to find out more about myself. Maybe I've taken this organization stuff too far . . .

—Warren Farrell, Ph.D.
Author, *Why Men Are The Way They Are* and
Women Can't Hear What Men Don't Say

Acknowledgments

I HAVE MANY PEOPLE TO THANK for their help in the preparation of this book. Diana Cunningham, Jessi Bromwell, and Deb McCown read for clarity, flow, and typos. Susan Davidson typed most passages. Valerie Davidson, age 14, gave Daddy the inspiration to complete the book.

Jill Alexander, the acquiring series editor and my managing editor, offered her usual blend of support, insight, and guidance. Thanks also to Amy Collins in Sales, Nancy True in Marketing and Sales, Gene Molter and Beth Gissinger in Publicity and Promotions, Stephanie McKenna in International Rights and Distribution, and Nancy Allen in Customer Service. Thanks to Scott Watrous for ensuring smooth operations and to Bob Adams for his ever-constant vision and excellence.

Thanks to subject matter experts Robert Fritz, Nancilee Wydra, Jim Cathcart, Nicholas Lemann, Dr. Wayne Dyer, Robert Levasseur, Jaclyn Kostner, Ph.D., Robert Cooper, Ph.D., Michael Gershon, M.D., Barbara Hemphill, Stephen Hawking, Ph.D., Don Aslett, and the late David McClelland Ph.D., Vilfredo Pareto, and Earl Nightingale.

Introduction

WHY SHOULD I GET ORGANIZED? Why bother? What for? Derek Bok, former president of Harvard University, achieved 15 minutes of fame just by saying, "If you think education is costly, try ignorance." If you think getting organized is time consuming, try disorganization.

If the places and spaces all around you are always cluttered, what are the potential consequences you might be experiencing? Do you feel overwhelmed by the never-ending lists of responsibilities and tasks that need to be completed? Are you caught up in a seemingly unyielding cycle of work that makes you feel as if you are always running behind? Do you find yourself brushing up against deadlines and sometimes completing projects after they are due? If you have answered yes to any of these questions, you may have just the right tool to help you become, and remain, more organized.

Consider the array of situations, places, and spaces (both mental and physical) in your work and life where it probably makes sense to be organized, such as:

- Attics
- Basements
- Cellars
- Closets
- Collections
- Accumulations
- Desktops

- Filing cabinets
- Garages
- Home and work offices
- Meetings
- Moving to a new location
- Cubicles
- Paper management
- Wardrobe

When you start listing everything, the list grows pretty long. You're probably wondering how you are going to tackle each of these areas. Fortunately, you only need to understand a few guiding principles and hands-on techniques to keep your life in order! And lucky you, all you need to know is in this nifty little volume. We're going to tackle getting organized head on!

Disorganization is costly—The negative effects of disorganization may be wreaking havoc on your career, though you may not even realize it. Or maybe you do realize it, but can't bear to think about it. Do you send a negative message to others? Are people reluctant to ask you for help? Are you regarded as someone who is not a team player? Do you end up leaving important tasks unfinished because you are not organized enough to complete them? Are you absent or tardy more than others in your organization?

Do you have an inability to let go? Does your disorganization represent an attempt to collect and retain pieces of the past? Does this backlog of outdated material hamper your ability to take advantage of current challenges? Does the clutter around you diminish your productivity? Do you feel guilty when you are not engaged in work-related activities? Are you putting in overtime more frequently than you'd prefer?

These are problems disorganized people know all too well. Beyond the negative effects disorganization may have on your career, also consider what it can do to your personal life. Some people believe that disorganization is possibly associated with anxieties or illness. If you suspect that your health and happiness could be at stake, it's time to face up to the task of getting organized.

Responding to Life

Becoming and staying organized take effort and thought, but they save time and offer peace of mind. Okay, a little peace of mind. The not-so-great paradox is that you expend time to save time. If it's helpful, think of getting organized as preparation "to respond to life."

Considering the sea of material goods, constant information, and endless communication that bombards everyone daily, getting organized is a growing problem for you, and you are probably retaining too many items—ones that you have overcollected and overfiled.

No one is born with organizational skills, particularly you, and everybody has to learn them along the way. When you do finally get organized, do you quit after a while, believing it's hopeless to live without the clutter and mess? The key to getting and remaining organized is recognizing how valuable it can be to have everything in order, and then making the changes necessary for cutting through the chaos. For many, it is a welcome relief to learn how long it will take; I estimate that, for most people, it is the equivalent of about three full weekends and four to five weeknights.

Q: Say, Jeff, why do some people avoid getting organized even when they lament their disorganization?

A: Beats me. Maybe they approach getting organized with fear and trepidation. Some people think imposing order on their life will somehow strip them of their inner essence or disturb their primal state. They become anxious about the thought of getting organized. Yet getting and remaining

organized is an essential element to a successful career
and, possibly, to a happy home life.

How organized are you? If your short answer is "don't ask,"
have I got a surprise for you: a short quiz. Please use a number
two soft lead pencil and keep your eyes on your own paper; you'll
only be cheating yourself . . . Now then, if you answer "yes" to any
of the following, drop everything and read the suggested tip.

1. Do you spend five minutes or more looking for a letter or document? It doesn't take that long to find one simple sheet of
   paper. Don't kid yourself. If you can't find it, you can't find it.
2. Are month-old papers on your desk? A desk is not a filing
   cabinet.
3. Do you have trouble finding a particular item in your desk that
   you use frequently? Maybe it's best left on top of your desk.
4. Do you feel that you could be organized if you only had
   more space? More space is seldom the answer; filing away
   or throwing away the nonessential is the best solution.
5. Do you have piles of newspapers and magazines you haven't
   been able to read? If you're thinking of reading these issues
   cover to cover, good luck. How about simply extracting the
   handful of articles that look most intriguing and letting go of
   the rest?
6. Did you ever find something at the bottom of a pile that you
   didn't know was there? You're liable to lose anything!
   Condense your piles by eliminating old papers and filing
   away important ones.

If none of the above quiz questions applied to you, congratula-
tions! You can start with tip #1. If all of the above questions applied
to you, it still makes sense to start with this tip, too!

Part One:

Embracing Powerful Perspectives

Relax: Organizing Is Not So Bad

IN THE 1950s AND THROUGHOUT THE 1960s AND 1970s, the Success Motivational Institute, Nightingale-Conant, and a host of other self-improvement businesses emerged. These organizations offered motivational programs designed to help listeners achieve personal goals, including how to get organized.

By the 1980s, dozens of companies had sprung up that offered cassettes, videos, and other materials on virtually all aspects of career and life. These aids ostensibly could help anyone get from point A to point B more efficiently. By the 1990s, such programs were offered via CD-ROM and through other digital and electronic formats.

Lack of scientific research in the field of human achievement, however, prompted many scholars and journalists to scoff at what the public was being told about self-improvement.

Dr. David McClelland of Harvard University was among the most prominent researchers to explore the potential connection between mental functioning and career or personal success. For several decades before his death in 1998, McClelland studied the potential links between what one thinks about and what one achieves.

McClelland was convinced that men and women of humble origins could break ranks and redesign their lives. Certainly, this is wonderful news for all who ever had a hankering to be all that they could be. Now, here's where you come in.

If you are reading this book, you are probably among those individuals who want to improve life by generating a routine of organization—whether you need improvement organizing your life at the office, at your home, or with your thoughts.

You have the power to set and achieve your goals of becoming and remaining organized, and to use this power to follow through in other aspects of your life. You have the ability to summon your own personal motivation to overcome the challenges and roadblocks in your path so that you may attain your desired level of organization. So, there go all your excuses . . .

Here's a new perspective: Getting things in order can be fun, or at least satisfying. If you've ever been to a hockey match and seen the Zamboni machine used between periods, then you've seen a creative approach to a chore. A driver climbs in and carefully circles the ice, laying a thin coat of water, which soon freezes, leaving the rink in brand-new condition—hard, smooth, clean, and ready for the play period. The drivers traditionally make one giant loop around the outermost area of the rink, and then come down the middle of the rink, creating two noticeably long semicircles.

In a winding fashion, the driver then completes one-half of the rink, moving closer toward the middle of the half he's currently working on. Then he swings over and completes the other side of the rink. When he's done, the entire floor of ice is smooth, gleaming, and ready for the players. Each organizing task you decide to tackle, no matter how insignificant or mundane, can become a challenging project, like the Zamboni's task. If you have to rearrange shelves, for example, make a game out of rearranging them efficiently. If you have to remove debris from your back deck, take it on as a challenge. In many instances, there is no single "right way" to do it, so proceed in a manner that is enjoyable to you.

No matter how you try to organize, you have the option of approaching the task in many different ways, and you will then be able to successfully monitor your own progress.

2

Learn Your ABCs

PONDER THIS: Why are you able to achieve the things you achieve? The three basic elements to any behavioral change are:

1. Antecedents
2. An action or behavior itself
3. The consequences of that action or behavior

These are the ABCs of behavioral change!

Suppose you're driving along a country road on a warm spring day. Suddenly, you see a stop sign. The sign is the antecedent. The behavior derived from this is you, in your car, stopping. As a consequence, you obey the law, avoiding the possibility of either an accident or an arrest resulting from driving through the stop sign. In short, you get to keep on driving!

Imagine this same situation, but with a different behavior. You see a stop sign (antecedent), and rather than stopping, your behavior is to ignore it and drive through it. What are the consequences? If no one is around, you might save a couple of seconds and continue on your way. But what if a police officer across the street sees you, stops you, gives you a ticket, and you lose your license? Or, maybe you get into a serious accident?

Antecedents precede behaviors, and behaviors precede consequences. When you recall major accomplishments, such as, being accepted to college, or landing your first job, you discover that these accomplishments follow the pattern of antecedent, behavior, and consequence: A, B, C.

When the consequences of your behavior are positive, your experience can be an antecedent for other people. For example, the date of the final exam is announced. So you get organized and begin studying a month in advance. You are well prepared to take the test, and as a consequence, you ace it. For you, it was a piece of cake. Your roommate realizes how well you've done. The next time he has an exam, he emulates your behavior and does well. He then buys you a whopper of a gift as a display of his gratitude.

Virtually every goal you've ever set, and every goal that you will set, is based upon some sort of antecedent. Recognition of opportunity and the fear of pain are the two fundamental antecedents for engaging in behaviors that lead to goal achievement. You proceed in goal-setting behavior based on either opportunity that you envision or pain that you wish to avoid. Pretty basic stuff, right?

This simple paradigm is complicated by the fact that each person's conception of opportunity for gain is multifaceted. In addition, the ways in which people seek to avoid pain are varied. These two fundamental antecedents are often intertwined in ways you may not realize. For example, if your quest is to become more organized at work, it might be for any one of the following opportunity-related reasons. You might wish to:

- Demonstrate competency
- Be recognized as an expert
- Improve your chances for advancement
- Get a pay increase
- Act as a team player
- Use less space at your desk, cubicle, or office
- Set an example in your department

At the same time, however, "avoidance of pain" may be a factor. You may try to:

- Avoid looking like you're swamped
- Comply with your boss's orders and avoid a reprimand
- Not spend so much time searching for misplaced things
- Not appear disorderly to visitors
- Avoid feeling inadequate

Perhaps your motivation stems from your perception that everyone else expects you to maintain an orderly desk, cubicle, or office. Maybe you crave having people regard you as being in control. Or, you want to get organized because you know there is someone out there who is convinced that you can't do it.

When you better understand your motivation for getting organized (the antecedent), you can then take the appropriate action (behavior) that will result in the desired achievement (consequence): A, B, C!

3 Capture Your Best Thoughts

CONSIDER HOW HARD IT IS TO GET STARTED on some organizing projects. Why risk being derailed by a disruption that need not have occurred at all? Regardless of how many times you are interrupted in a typical day or hour, recognize that the interruption itself is not the major culprit. You ask, then, what is? The major culprit is misdirection, dawdling, and downtime on the path returning to where you were and what you were doing. So, my friend, do all you can to prevent interruptions from occurring in the first place.

Hold the phones, bar the door, post a notice, and safeguard in general your time and efforts whenever you're engaged in organizing a space or place in your career or personal life. You'll finish that much sooner and feel good about what you've accomplished, or at least you'll feel more neutral, than if you constantly stop for the little things like the telephone, e-mail, or to actually investigate Internet popup ads and their promise of fame and fortune.

To tap the level of brainwave activity where you can think profoundly, meditate, go for a walk in the woods, or take some other action to vanquish noise and distractions. Some people choose to go on vacation, take a drive, or take a break just by sitting on the porch or sofa. Many people have tremendous moments of insight and resolve while mountain climbing (or so I've been told). Others are able to merely sit in a favorite chair and wait for inspiration to spring forth. Some are able to use commuting time to great effect. The thoughts generated during such times have potentially significant value, but they are useless if not harnessed.

Once you've found a quiet space, literally or figuratively, determining what you want to achieve is largely a question of values. What type of project are you willing to commit to? What areas merit your time and energy?

Depending on the nature of your work, your thoughts might be among your most valuable assets to determine where to devote your attention. While many people have recurring thoughts throughout the day, some, if not most of these thoughts go unrecorded. Do you take time to organize your thoughts? Do you remember your ideas, and how to relay them, when they are original and creative? If not, you could be shortchanging yourself in major ways without realizing it.

Organizing your thoughts may have direct applicability to your assigned projects, and can only help you. Some may seem amorphous for now, but later, they may take on a more compelling nature. Often, the types of thoughts that get shortchanged, i.e., not recorded, are those directly related to staying organized.

While you can't act on the majority of your innovative thoughts immediately, you can organize them for later action. In a notebook, palm-top computer, or on your hard drive, set up a file where you can park the seemingly random thoughts which occur to you throughout the workday. Some people find it useful to use an electronic organizer. Some use a white board to record notes and later save them to a hard drive. Others might use the traditional calendar planner, jotting down important notes or dates. Use the back of an envelope or a napkin if that's all that you have to work with at the moment. Then there are those who send reminder e-mails out to a couple dozen of their closest associates, friends, or family. Scanners, copiers, printers, and other office equipment can be used to record, assemble, and review tasks. Shouldn't you take advantage of these simple ways to organize your busy mind?

Ever since I began using a tape recorder to dictate reminders, I have found that dictating my thoughts on tape, having someone else transcribe the tape, and then saving these thoughts on my hard drive has made a world of difference. (See tips #23 and #48 for more information on dictating.)

Suppose you're in a meeting and it suddenly strikes you that buying a certain type of notepad, or arranging your desk in a new way could make a dramatic, no, make that a drastic improvement in your efficiency. If you don't write down the thought, if you leave it marinating in your busy mind, it tends to overcook and slip away. Ultimately, you never act on the thought, and you continue to operate in the same ineffective way.

The late Earl Nightingale, a renowned motivational speaker and author, once said, "Ideas are like slippery fish. Unless you write them down, they are going to slip away." The sad reality about novel ideas is that most of those that slip away will not come back. What a bummer! You will not have the same moment of inspiration twice. They are what Professor Stephen Hawking, celebrated astrophysicist and author of *A Brief History of Time,* calls singularities, one-time events. It's up to you to make the most of them.

Determine "Who Created That?"

IN HIS BOOK, *THE PATH OF LEAST RESISTANCE,* author Robert Fritz suggests that you ask yourself a critical question when you're faced with a challenging situation. The question is: Who created that?

More times than you probably care to admit, most of the situations you encounter in your life, and all of those related to staying organized, were created by you. Take your house, for example. Can you name a room, a space within a room, or even a single drawer for which you (or anyone else who lives with you) are not responsible? Does the wind blow so strangely through your windows that closets become disorganized? Do gremlins visit each night and mess up everything while you're asleep? I think not.

When you honestly confront an issue, you're bound to concede that you created the disorganization in your work and home. There's no one else to blame. I'm sure you're familiar with a situation that has occurred when coworkers have changed or moved around things that once had order. At home, certainly, a spouse or significant other, children, or other relatives could have a major hand in the disorganization that you face. In all instances, you, being a person of influence, have considerable control over the level of impact that others have on your organizing efforts.

If your child's bedroom is a perpetual disaster area, i.e., it never ceases to look like it was hit by a hurricane, flood, and earthquake all at once, that doesn't mean that every other room in the house has to be a pigsty. It also doesn't mean that any of your places and spaces in the house should ever be disorganized as a result of your child's activities.

If you are a neatnik and you married a messy type, you've got a challenge. The "Felix and Oscar" syndrome may be cute in the movie and follow-up television program *The Odd Couple,* but this is not the case in real life. Two neatniks or two messy people will get along far better than a neatnik and a messy person. (Hey, I didn't create the situation; I'm only reporting the news.)

If you work or live with "perpetually disorganized" people, you begin to see that your attraction to or tolerance of messy types contributes to the accumulation of organizing tasks. This observation is not meant to convince you to abandon your mate or seek a new job, but merely to emphasize that you are the person in control in your life. If work, home, or any other aspect of your life is not organized at a level that is comfortable for you, remember who created that situation, and choose to take control.

5

Make Profound Choices

YOU'RE SITTING IN TRAFFIC ON THE INTERSTATE HIGHWAY. It's a sweltering day in August and your car's air conditioner conks out. Do you feel justified in being irritated? You could be, but more positive choices are available.

You could hum a favorite song. You could choose to acknowledge the charmed life you're leading, or remember that you've been stuck before, and when reflecting on what happened the last time, recall that the situation proved to be of no real consequence. You could be glad that you live in this country, about what's planned for dinner this evening, or that your children are taking you someplace fun for your birthday. As Dr. Wayne Dyer, bestselling author and psychologist, teaches, how you elect to feel is always your choice. The act of choosing is a simple, but powerful technique that will aid you in becoming and remaining organized.

By making important choices, you automatically redirect yourself to accept that there is nothing you must do. Everything is based on your choice. If you choose to keep working on some task, even one assigned to you, this personal decision is made in the present moment, and not based on a prior agenda. The new sense of control over your own life yields a tremendous sense of inner harmony.

What are some of the powerful thinking techniques you can keep in mind as you decide to increase your capacity for becoming and remaining organized? Glad you asked:

- I choose to easily become and remain organized
- I choose to regard getting organized as a fun and worthwhile activity
- I choose to easily take control of my spaces
- I choose to maintain clarity when facing organizing challenges
- I choose to constantly recognize the areas of life where I'm a master of staying organized
- I choose to easily learn new methods of becoming organized
- I choose to associate with people who are highly organized and will serve as role models, mentors, and teachers
- I choose to approach disorganized situations with calmness and clarity

- I choose to readily reward myself for my organization victories
- I choose to feel good about the effort I put forth to get organized
- I choose to embrace challenging situations methodically and effectively
- I choose to be an overall master of personal organization

To reinforce the choices you make, write or type your choices and post them, or record them on a cassette and play them back.

How many choices can you make in one sitting? Make a few or many; there is no limit. Choose what feels right for you, and keep choosing. While you're waiting in a bank line, run through your decisions. If you notice yourself wavering, recall the new behavior or feeling that you've chosen. You can choose to overcome rituals that no longer support you, or you can make choices that will help mold you into an expert at organizing your life.

6

Live and Actually Learn

A NEW IDEA IS SUCH A RARE THING. We often simply imitate what we hear and read. You can, however, make choices that are not congruent with your history. If, for example, you have never felt that you had an affinity for becoming and remaining organized, you can make the decision to change that!

In a study published in the 1996 Annual Review of Psychology, researchers at Tel Aviv University and the University of Waterloo in Ontario found that:

> *. . . people less able to relate the person of the past to the person they are now may be at greater psychological risk, because they are thinking only in the present and their view of the future may not be developed.*

In other words, if you're not able to recognize how you've changed since the past, you're likely to allow your past to unduly influence what you do next. If you walk around saying, "I've never been good at organizing" and fail to acknowledge how you've changed over the years, or if you can't recall some of your recent organizational triumphs, you're needlessly putting yourself down. You should properly reward yourself for the organizational challenges you have overcome!

Getting stuck in the past is a major problem for entire nations as well as individuals. "Many international conflicts have their roots in divergent interpretations of the past," say the researchers from Tel Aviv University and the University of Waterloo in Ontario. (Think about how much time is still devoted to arguing about the Civil War, which ended seven score years ago!) So your problem may spring from the fact that people frequently react to the present as if they were still living in the past. For many people, "The past represents the context in which people acquire knowledge about future possibilities." Too many people formulate their forecasts from what they recall of the past and what they perceive in the present. Therefore, it behooves you to draw accurately upon your past, and note what's different about today. Only then can you make clear and confident choices about what you want in the future.

Did you get all that? So, you want to be more organized? It's within your power! Rather than living life looking through a rear view mirror, go where you've never gone before to set and reach goals that might have once seemed beyond your ability. Perhaps, the power to achieve them was within you all along.

"Work Smarter" for Real

YOU'VE PROBABLY BEEN ADVISED BEFORE to "work smarter not harder." This sage wisdom is routinely dispensed to people who need to become and remain organized. If you had precise information, a team of knowledgeable advisors, and an abundance of relevant resources, I suppose you'd have the opportunity to "work smarter, not harder." But what does "work smarter," actually mean in the real world?

Was Thomas Edison working smarter when he tried and failed to identify a suitable filament more than 8,000 times before creating a commercially viable light bulb? After he finally found the right filament, did his IQ suddenly rise? Working longer and being open to new ideas can lead to working smarter. With hard work, you can learn about your subject and develop more efficient techniques.

Simply telling someone to work smarter is not enough. I believe that the true message behind the adage "work smarter not harder" is take a little time to reflect on what you want to accomplish. Perhaps you can work smarter by striving to be a little more organized each day. Then you can start heading in a positive direction, and assemble the requisite resources to finish a project. You increase the odds that you'll be able to accomplish the job more quickly and easily.

A profound way to "work smarter" is to follow your inner wisdom. There is far more to your instincts, intuition, or gut feelings than you might think. Scientists in the field of neuro-cardiology have discovered a "brain in the heart." Comprised of more than 40,000 neurons of various types, along with a complex network of neuro-transmitters, proteins, and support cells, it acts independently of the head. "This heart brain," says Robert Cooper, Ph.D., "is as large as many key areas of the thinking brain and sufficiently sophisticated to rate as a brain in its own right."

Heartbeats aren't merely mechanical pumping pulses. They have an intelligent language that influences how we perceive and react to the world. Each and every heartbeat is linked to the thinking brain and affects both branches of the autonomic nervous system, continually influencing our perceptions and awareness. Cooper says, "The heart is not only open to new possibilities, it actively scans for them, ever seeking new, intuitive understanding."

But hold on! Pioneering research by physiologists and gastroenterologists indicates that there is also another "brain" inside the intestines. Known as the "enteric nervous system," it is independent of, and interconnected with the brain in the cranium, according to Michael Gershon, M.D., Chair, Anatomy and Cell Biology at Columbia University.

Cooper observes that, "gut instincts are real and warrant listening to." For most of the organizing challenges you will face, you probably have a strong idea as to how to best proceed. Often, you don't follow your own inner wisdom. You let yourself be pressured by external sources that, in retrospect, offer little contribution.

The solution: Rely on your instincts more routinely. In other words, use all of your brains! Decisions based on instincts and intuition rapidly and automatically encompass all of your life experiences and acquired knowledge. If you're figuring out how to organize something, it's often okay to simply start and let your intuition guide you. Every aspect of your being goes into making a decision based on instinct or intuition. Your decision isn't whimsical, random, or foolish.

Heed Pareto and His Principle

IN 1897, ITALIAN ECONOMIST VILFREDO PARETO discovered a relationship between effort and result now known as the Pareto Principle or the 80/20 rule. He found that 80 percent of what someone achieves is derived from 20 percent of the time that individual expends. Results, outputs, or rewards tend to come from a small proportion of the inputs or efforts directed toward achieving them. Specifically, 20 percent of your organizing efforts will yield 80 percent of your desired effect. Imagine that—1/5 of what you do accounts for 4/5 of what you accomplish!

Unhappily, most people devote 80 percent of their efforts, which only yields 20 percent of their returns! Macro effort, micro result—know the feeling? The key to effectiveness is to continually identify the 20 percent of your activities that are most important, those that yield the greatest results. For example, straightening the pens on your desk may be satisfying, but it likely doesn't improve the quality of your work. On the other hand, carefully adding new information onto your contact management software could be the lifeblood of your business or career.

When the Pareto Principle was specifically applied to business, startling observations followed. Within an insurance agency, for example, 20 percent of the agents were found to produce approximately 80 percent of the sales. In a hardware store, 20 percent of the floor space accounted for 80 percent of the profits. In an accounting firm, 20 percent of the clients generated 80 percent of the revenues. It made sense for such firms to find lucrative, long-term clients, to focus their energy and attention on the most profitable percentage, and have the strength to let go of the weaker clientele.

Similarly, it makes sense for you to focus the precious time you have for organizing in those areas where it will do you the most good. Your needs will differ from others even in your own company or family. A logical way to streamline your efforts is to concentrate on those areas where breakdowns are all too frequent. These problem areas are easy to spot. They're signified by time wasted, lost opportunities, accidents, and other negative indicators. In others words, give up pretending that dealing in minutia will generate large rewards.

Forget about the "Right Mood"

WHEN YOU WAIT UNTIL YOU ARE "IN THE MOOD" to get organized, you run the risk that the right mood will come at an inopportune time or even not at all! Consider the professional writer who steadfastly maintains a writing quota of a certain number of words per day. The writer who vows to complete 1,800 words by noon each day will complete 9,000 words in a typical workweek, and 36,000 words in four weeks. Whether or not the writer "feels like it," the daily writing quota ensures the achievement of a desired output.

You may argue that forcing yourself to meet a word count serves little purpose if the writing isn't good. However, writers who set such quotas tend to self-correct as they proceed. Therefore, the words written on any given day are roughly as effective, coherent, and on the mark as the words written randomly on any other day. Occasionally, the daily performance level dips a bit, but this is offset by other days when the performance level exceeds expectations. Similarly, you may accomplish the most when you are "in the mood" to organize, but it is important to focus on your efforts even when you are feeling rather unenthusiastic.

Getting organized requires less motivation than being a professional writer. You can set your daily quota of organizing tasks at a low level and still achieve good results. By doing something—regardless of your mood—you're farther ahead than if you did nothing. You may not manage to complete a task on your first attempt. However, it's to your benefit to at least try and start.

Peering from the peak of one mountain, the next mountain doesn't look so far. When you're down in the valley, though, hiking and cursing through a dark, entangling rhododendron thicket with a dull machete, reaching the next peak can seem extremely difficult even if you're already more than halfway to the top. So when you're making your way through a cluttered file cabinet, it may seem as if your task is insurmountable. Yet, with only a tiny bit of effort, you can progress farther along than if you hadn't tried at all.

Stop believing that you have to "feel like getting organized" and instead, proceed based upon your desire for results, such as tidying the top drawer of your desk.

Reward Thyself

IF KEEPING THINGS ORGANIZED DOESN'T COME EASY FOR YOU, use basic psychology to increase the probability that you'll achieve one success after another: Reward yourself.

People who are reasonably adept at rewarding others for a job well done are often curiously deficient when it comes to rewarding themselves. If you have children, you may pride yourself in giving them positive reinforcement when they have demonstrated good behavior. How often, however, do you practice positive reinforcement with yourself? Use this system to start rewarding yourself for all the hard work you've done!

The key to making your system of self-rewards work is to:

1. Make the reward commensurate with the effort (i.e., you don't buy yourself a Mazda for straightening out the bathroom).
2. Give yourself the reward soon after your accomplishment. If you finish cleaning the yard, there is little psychological connection to any reward you give yourself three weeks later.
3. Form a solid connection in your mind between your effort and the reward, and then use that as motivation to get started on whatever else needs to be organized.

Some people find it helpful to identify the reward in advance. If you decide to tackle that filing cabinet you've been ignoring for so long, and you know that after your magnificent triumph you're going to treat yourself to a new pair of shoes, you can form a clear image of the reward as you proceed. This helps particularly if you feel your energy lagging or you begin to lose sight of your goal.

Some individuals, including me, prefer to determine the reward spontaneously. Once I've "aced" some organizing task, I walk around my office or home with the mini-mission of stumbling into something I enjoy doing. It could be picking up a favorite magazine, visiting a favorite Web site, having a snack, or even taking a snooze.

A sparse word to those widely prone to gluttony: Be cautious that the majority of your rewards for jobs well done are not related to food. It's too easy to slip into the trap of continually rewarding yourself with some sweet, yummy snack. Even if you employ healthful snacks, such as carrot sticks, an apple, or a rice cake, you still run the risk of equating accomplishment with food consumption. I'm not saying to rule out food as one of your rewards; simply make it one of an array of potential rewards.

Master the mini-reward: If your organizing project is sizable and/or long-term in nature, divide your task into segments, with planned mini-rewards along the way to keep you going.

Suppose you're organizing your garage, a task you've dreaded since right after the garage was built. Your conservative estimate is that the project will take at least three hours. Nine small, self-generated rewards at 20-minute intervals might help you persevere in what otherwise might seem to be an entirely arduous task.

As you proceed, sometimes you get into a rhythm or a flow and have no need to stop after 20 minutes. That's fine; simply pause when pausing feels right and appropriately reward yourself. Your ability to positively reinforce your behavior at periodic junctures as you proceed is vital.

Maybe you're the type of person who wants to break only after an hour, or you prefer to have only one break in the middle. For some tasks, I know I won't be satisfied until I have completed the whole darn thing, and that if I pause, I will lose impetus. In such cases, I regard completion of the entire project as a reward in itself, and when done, believe me, I have no problem taking a run, watching a favorite show, going to a movie, or figuring out some other type of reward.

Sometimes you are making great progress on a huge project when, despite your best efforts, your energy starts to wane. You can use a variety of self-generated rewards to keep going and give yourself periodic breaks and other critical time-outs. Nevertheless, you will encounter some tasks upon which you can proceed no farther that day or at least for the time being. Here, it is critical to know when to stop.

Many books will tell you how to get started, and how to keep in motion once you have gotten started. Knowing when to stop can be as important as anything else on your path to becoming and remaining organized.

If you're mentally or physically exhausted, and you induce yourself to proceed past some optimal point, you may actually diminish your willingness and ability to pick up on the project again later that day, or the next day, or whenever you had intended to resume working on it. Especially for larger organizing projects, knowing when to stop can be one of the most subtle, key components in pursuit of your desired end result.

What are some of the telltale signs that you have hit the wall and it is best not to proceed any farther for now? Here are a few:

- After having taken several breaks and giving yourself appropriate rewards, you find yourself simply going through the motions and not making any real progress
- You start making costly errors
- Your productivity drops off
- You have completely lost track of your mission
- Staying on the project any longer would jeopardize your ability to give your attention to other important tasks and responsibilities
- You are missing a critical resource and while it is admirable to attempt to make do, no further significant progress is expected
- You become so disagreeable (in the case of working with others), it makes sense to reconvene later today, tomorrow, or at some other scheduled time

Finally, if you can't remember what you're working on, give yourself a break!

Part Two:

Enveloping Provocative Practices

Forsake Excuses for Not Becoming Organized

EVEN WHEN YOU KNOW IT MAKES SENSE TO BEGIN A TASK, too many excuses keep you from getting started. Here are some wimpy ones for not getting your hands dirty:

1.   "I have been meaning to." If this sounds familiar, then make getting completely organized a high-ranking item in your life. See tip #18.

2.   "I have never been good at organizing . . ." This is of no consequence. All is forgiven. Those "not good" at organizing believe that somehow things "simply get out of order" or "get lost." The difference between people who are "good at organizing" and those who are "not good" is that people who are organized recognize the effort required to maintain organization.

3.   "I don't know how to get started." Keep reading.

4.   "I have so many other things to do." Of course you do; you will for the rest of your life. After getting organized, however, the other things you "have to do" will more directly support your priorities and goals, and you will have a clearer image of the connection between your work and your achievements. See tip #19.

5.   "Organizing will take too much time." For most people, it takes three weekends and several weeknights. Okay, maybe you need longer than that! Go back and reread the introduction and keep considering what disorganization has cost you.

6.   "I don't see any value in organizing." Many aspects of people's lives are already organized, whether you realize it or not.

Now you are about to enhance personal control, which has great value, by extending the procedures you may already be using.

7.   "It makes me anxious; I don't feel that I am accomplishing that much." If you only toss unnecessary files and papers, creating more space, you will be accomplishing a great deal.

When you're able to forsake excuses about getting organized, you open yourself up to some highly worthwhile achievements. Thereafter, getting organized emerges as a regular and vital preliminary step to the things you want to accomplish.

Defeat Perfectionism

AT TIMES, STRIVING FOR PERFECTION IS APPROPRIATE: A medical doctor performing a complex operation, a pilot landing a jumbo jet plane, and a police detective investigating a murder should all strive to do the best possible job. Yet, even for people in these professions, there are situations where perfectionism is unnecessary, unwarranted, and overly time-consuming.

For the doctor, a bandaging job after an operation, regardless of how neat it is, should stop bleeding. For the airline pilot, a landing where one wheel touches down a half second after the other will not diminish the quality of the flight. For the police detective, not interviewing an eleventh witness after interviewing ten witnesses who independently corroborate each other's observations will probably be okay.

Studies show that the additional time you spend to take a project from the 95 percent mark to the 100 percent mark is, in most cases, not worth it. Striving for perfection, i.e., ensuring that the final 5 percent is correctly done, often takes as much time as the initial 95 percent of effort required! Gosh, no wonder it felt so difficult!

When giving instructions to your staff, if you give them nine or ten suggestions on how to effectively do a job, but you forget one or two suggestions, they will still have plenty to work with. Conversely, if you strive to give them every great suggestion you can offer, the time and effort that you expend may be unnecessary, and the marginal value of the extra suggestions for your staff may not be nearly worth the effort.

In your own work, there are countless instances throughout the day when not being "perfect" makes more sense from a practical standpoint than striving for perfection. If you're turning in a report, and your department is structured so that the production team does the copyediting, it doesn't pay for you to slave over a 100 percent grammatically and tactically correct report. When you're assembling data to make a decision, if you wait until you have reams of information, the opportunity before you may pass. What's more, if you collect too much data, you can become more confused than informed! You may even become buried in enough paper to create a new organizational nightmare!

Many decisions can be made based on instinct and intuition and still turn out fine. This is because when you're making a decision, although you may not realize it, you're actually drawing upon all of the information to which you have ever been exposed. Let go of the quest to overcollect.

Hereafter, assemble the body of information necessary to help you feel comfortable with your decision, but do no more than that. Likewise, look for other opportunities throughout the workday when a 90 to 95 percent effort will be fine.

13

Start Simply

HAVE YOU EVER FALLEN INTO THIS TRAP? You accumulate a pile of stuff that is begging to be organized, but you have trouble tackling the task because you overcomplicate things. Maybe you have a streak of perfectionism that prompts you to believe that the task is going to take more time than is necessary to get comfortably organized. Perhaps you seek to arrange items in the most judicious order possible.

If any of the above types of thinking plague your ability to get organized, banish them to the far, far corners of your mind and accept this general principle:

Sometimes the best type of organization is the simplest.

Consider an everyday example. Your desk is a disaster. You've looked at it day after day, and you dread the thought of having to put everything in order. You may even be secretly hoping that a tornado will come tearing through your office and carry everything away so that you don't have to face the mess. Yet, deep down, you know that it will be to your extreme advantage to get your desk in order. Why not allow yourself a simple start, thereby decreasing the pressure on yourself and increasing the probability of your success?

A quick first step would be to round up all the pens and pencils that populate your desk. Put them in a pencil holder, can, or container.

Next, grab all the Post-It pads, note pads, and scraps of paper that contain any vital information, be it an address, a phone number, or a Web site. Then, decide here and now to do the following:

1.   Enter the information on your hard drive in a folder that is designed to be a catchall for such tidbits of information, or,

2.   Lay down these Post-It pads and scraps of information on the copier to create one or two collective pages to be neatly filed, or folded and parked in the corner of your desk for quick reference. (Clue: If you have all such tidbits in one place, you have a far better chance of finding and using them as needed.) Ideally, you don't let such tidbits pile up to begin with; however, if this is a habit, you are probably going to keep doing this without realizing you're doing it.

Now, collect all the file folders on your desk. The file folders represent tasks or projects that you'll be tackling. Make sure each file folder includes the appropriate materials, then refile all the file folders except for those that you will be working with this morning or this afternoon.

Next, gather up any books, reports, or other large documents, and place them on the appropriate shelves. If you need specific pages from such documents, copy them on a copier, put those pages in the corresponding file folder, and put the original books, documents, and reports away.

By now you're probably well on your way to becoming more organized. Clearing your desk is not that big of a deal. Make it simple. Tackle similar items such as pens and pencils all at once, then go on to the next type of item, and the next, until the desk is back under your control. You can do it. You will even live to tell about it.

Organize According to Your Milestones

ATTENTION RECENT HIGH SCHOOL AND COLLEGE GRADUATES: After you finished school, it's understandable that career-oriented goals begin to predominate. Will you get a job? Will it be a good job? Will it be at a decent salary? Will you have to relocate? You probably embarked upon a course of study that prepared you for a specific line of work. Many people, however, haven't done this.

The best time to get organized about your career ambitions is before you graduate from school—a significant milestone. The more time you give yourself to plan careers or lifetime goals, the better your chances are of success.

If you started getting organized about where you want to work and what you want to do the day after you graduated, you may have found yourself underemployed, underpaid, and undervalued. You may have even found yourself unemployed. The graduation milestone is sufficiently noteworthy for most people to prepare for what they want to do afterward. You can harness that same sense of clarity and feeling of unity as other milestones come into range. Everyone has milestones in his or her life. Do any of these ring a bell for you?

- Your new job
- Marriage
- Buying a house and relocating
- Having children
- Selecting a day-care facility

- Going back to school
- Saving for your children's education
- Caring for your parents
- Retiring
- Traveling
- Coping with health problems

You can utilize these milestones as aids in your quest to become organized. Pretend you're approaching your 40th birthday. What sort of physical shape do you want to be in? In your office, what files are not worth retaining? What files need to be created?

You turn 40 only once. Milestones and events need not be of the once-per-lifetime variety. There are recurring events throughout the year, within particular seasons, and in the course of a month, that can serve as useful markers. On your quest to become more organized, your assignment is to recognize the value and practicality of acknowledging a wide variety of approaching milestones and events. Hereafter, use them as rallying points to spur your efforts. Let's look at two such milestones.

Relocating

With all of humankind's scientific, medical, and technological breakthroughs, you'd expect that someone would do something about the onerous task of relocating! Most people change residences after their college graduation, marriage, an increase in income, etc. Yet, there doesn't seem to be any way around loading and unloading every single thing you own, item by item, and box by box, into a car or truck. You can hire people, but the process of moving is no less upsetting. There are address cards to fill out, phone numbers to change, bills to reconcile, utility companies to call, and a ton of other activities to manage.

Moving does demand a high level of organization, at least at the outset of, and directly following, the move. You have to decide whether particular items will be transported, sold, or given away. This forces you to make decisions you wouldn't otherwise have to, especially if you were in the middle of a long-term lease and not considering relocating.

Beyond the physical move itself, there's something about the moving process that facilitates order. If you're married or living with a significant other, a move can be a wonderful time to mutually reorganize your possessions and living space. "We're not keeping that ratty old couch!" Perhaps you agree to let your partner have more space in the new location, or you both agree to set up a home gym. This is the opportunity to decide on exactly how you want to arrange your new home.

I had a friend in college who used to work for Amtrak in Washington, D.C. During his youth, he told me, his father worked for a *Fortune* 500 manufacturer and was frequently relocating to assume new positions. Because the family moved every couple of years, they made decisions about what to retain and what to toss. In the new location, they frequently lived in a clutter-free, streamlined home. When his family settled down for the long haul in a Southern Connecticut suburb, even after many years passed, they still maintained an organized, clutter-free household. This notion appealed to me long before I became a conference and convention speaker on the topic of having more breathing space and less clutter in your life. It was a pleasure to visit, unlike other friends' houses that were strewn with stuff in every room. I'm not saying you have to move frequently to maintain a clutter-free home. However, it certainly helps. The next time you move, recognize that a whole new opportunity for organizing your space comes with it.

Organizing Before and After a Job Change

Relocation can occur in life without actually moving from one place to another. Seeking a new job may be the start of an occupational relocation. Starting a job, whether or not you are currently employed, represents a variety of challenges. As emotionally nerve-racking and mentally draining looking for a job can be, it's one of the fundamental opportunities you'll have in life to get organized. When else do you have clear, uninterrupted stretches of time for determining exactly what's important in your life and career?

Perhaps you got fired or left your previous job under less than pleasant circumstances. Maybe you're new in the workplace and have never had a career position. You may be reentering the career world after many years. In any case, you're where you are for a reason and you have a marvelous opportunity to set your sights on what is most appropriate, challenging, and enjoyable for you. Clarity can help you get a job that is more consistent and more aligned with what you want to do in life and where you want to be at your age.

You may encounter other career milestones that naturally and spontaneously prompt you to reorganize. These include a large pay increase, your appointment to a special/high office, or your election as an officer in your professional association or group. A noncareer related milestone could include being asked to serve on a special committee supporting your town council.

When any of these kinds of events occur, given the new situation, you may find it fitting and appropriate to reexamine your office, your files, or your life. Hereafter, whether you are moving to a new location, a new place of employment, or a new stage in your life, take advantage of those opportunities and reorganize.

15

Handle Tough Things First

IF YOU FAIL TO FILE YOUR TAXES ON TIME, send cards out too late, shop for presents at the last minute, or struggle with desk drawers that are jam-packed with garbage, then it is in your best interest to change the way you handle such tasks. Any time you have control over the sequence in which you tackle responsibilities, handle the seemingly unpleasant elements first. If you save what you like to do for last, and handle the unpleasant things such as housekeeping tasks first, you maintain order a bit longer.

It sounds so easy, but why do people resort to old, unproductive ways of approaching their day? Bad habits or routine behavior have far more of an impact on daily activities than we might imagine. Research shows that the more an individual engages in a particular behavior, the stronger the neuronal pathways in that person's brain become, which encourages them to continue the behavior. If you allow piles to build up in your work area, as time marches on, you will keep on creating the clutter.

If you're involved in the same exercise regime or lack thereof, chances are, you'll continue on that same path. Alarmingly (at least to me!), research shows that if you continue living by these habits long enough, your ability to change literally decreases.

As you get older, decades of habitual behavior, habitual thought patterns, and a habitual life all but ensure that your capacity for change in the years to come will be a fraction of what it might have been 10, 20, and 30 years ago. This does not mean you can't change. Chances are, however, that you will need extraordinary motivation, such as your boss telling you to straighten up your desk or else!

It is an axiom of life that if you're seeking to develop a new habit, the best possible time to begin is now. The false promise of beginning something next week or next month is a disguised form of procrastination. The energy and anxiety that you invest in putting off an activity can consume more energy than required to perform the activity. Contemplating a change does have value, but germination has more value. So often the changes that you are resisting require less effort, energy, and time than you think.

The longer it's been since you attempted to get organized, the more likely you are to encounter steeper challenges. If procrastination is your enemy, then action is your friend. Remember the findings of Mr. Newton—a body in motion tends to stay in motion. As such, the tiniest action toward getting organized can start you on a winning path. It's definitely preferable to taking no action at all. A small action could consist of clearing your desk, making a purchase, finding a helper, visiting a key Web site, or prioritizing tasks.

Immerse Yourself for 60 Seconds

ONE OF THE MOST EFFECTIVE TECHNIQUES YOU CAN USE, true to the title of this book, is to engage in organizing activities for one minute at a time.

Suppose your office at work is a disaster area. You don't want to begin turning things around. Actually, you dread the task. Promise yourself that you will engage in an organizing activity for a single minute. You can set a timer or look at the clock on the wall, whatever works for you.

For 60 seconds, straighten up whatever you can. In the course of a minute, maybe you can only tackle one area. Conceivably, you can handle two or three items. Put away or discard extraneous items and neaten up any portion of your desk that will contribute to your overall quest.

Bzzzzzzz. At the end of 60 seconds, honoring your promise to yourself, stop and return to whatever you were doing previously.

Depending on the time of day, when the spirit moves you again later that morning or afternoon, return to your one minute routine. For 60 seconds, organize some part of your office. As unpalatable as the task may be, by engaging in it for only 60 seconds, you'll make some progress and feel better about yourself.

As with other techniques presented throughout this book, you'll find that after 60 seconds, you often don't want to stop. The momentum of your efforts carries on to the next minute and the next. As this happens, be supportive of yourself. Let yourself "go with the flow." Believe me, you'll stop when you want to, have to, or are too tired to proceed. Still, it's amazing how much one minute's worth of straightening up can do for most of the places and spaces in your life.

I've seen people clear out and reorganize a desk drawer in a minute or so. I have observed others who rescue their desktops from overflow in 60 seconds or less. I've witnessed others clear away shelf space or simply make a path through their offices during these 60 second campaigns. You'll never know how much you can accomplish during this time until you try. So try it; you might like it!

Ask Yourself "Will It Be Any Easier Later?"

WHEN YOU FIND YOURSELF FACING A PILE that needs to be organized, ask yourself a key question: "Will it be any easier to handle later?" Will organizing the pile somehow miraculously be less of a task in the future than it is right now? If the chore will be significantly easier at some point in the foreseeable future, then you may remain in a state of relative disorganization, secure in the knowledge that you will put things in order later.

About 99 times out of 100, however, the best time to tackle an organization task is right now! Later, the mess before you is likely to be worse. Piles grow higher. Files grow thicker. Stuff accumulates! Have you noticed?

By asking yourself if it will be easier to handle the task later, you automatically create a personal incentive to deal with it now, independent of what your mood happens to be. Whether it's disassembling the pile, reducing the size of the file, organizing the dining room tabletop, tackling the car glove compartment, or managing other spaces or places, getting organized is nearly always an easier task if you get started sooner.

What if asking, "Will it be any easier later?" does not serve as a great prompt to initiate your organizing task? Perhaps you have a procrastination, not an organizing, problem. As such, you'll be well served by my book *The 60 Second Procrastinator* (Adams Media, 2003), which offers 60 tips on overcoming procrastination. Many of them will give you that "kick-in-the-pants" start that you need and probably want.

Identify What's Thwarting You

If you find yourself completely unable to get started on a task, it may be because a legitimate obstacle or a temporary roadblock hampers you. Your excuse may actually be, drum roll . . . valid. The task may well prove to be easier later! It happens. Perhaps the organizing task is too big for you to handle alone and you need help. Maybe you don't have the right tools or equipment. Perhaps you lack the budget or monetary resources realistically required to do the job properly. Maybe this is not a good time to start due to weather conditions or environmental factors.

What if a forthcoming event renders your efforts temporarily futile? Suppose you desperately want to clean and reorganize your car. It's become so disorganized you want to howl in the night. Tomorrow, however, you're taking your daughter and two of her friends to the state fair. They're going to track dirt and food particles in and out of the car. They're going to accumulate banners, posters, stickers, and stuffed toys. Someone is bound to spill a drink or crush an oily French fry deep into your carpet. You are likely to find popcorn pieces and cotton candy trapped in the crevices of your seats. Are you visualizing a strong picture of this?

Would it make more sense to clean and organize your car now, or the day after taking a group of kids to the state fair? You guessed it, postponing your organizing efforts for a day or two is a better use of your time and tends to yield greater peace of mind. Who wants to whip the interior of the car into shape only to have it spoiled a day later, necessitating further efforts?

Do the kids actually care if they ride in a clean car or not? Do they even notice? For this and similar situations, you're better off waiting until after the event and then proceeding with your organizational plan. Identify what's thwarting your efforts at getting organized. If a more appropriate start time emerges, yield to it.

Organize Based on Your Priorities

LIVING A DISORGANIZED, CLUTTER-FILLED LIFE requires no particular skill—anyone can get the hang of it. Who is the most likely to be unorganized? Those who haven't identified their priorities and established supporting goals.

To organize effectively, it helps if you identify your priorities. Otherwise, you're organizing without a goal. Priorities are broad elements of life. They are so basic that you can often misplace them somewhere in your go-go schedule. Start identifying your priorities, and you'll realize that much of the clutter you have collected does not serve you or support your priorities. Much of what you've assembled in the places and spaces of your life is useless!

The procedure that follows is simple and direct and will help you to establish priorities.

1. Write down everything that is important to you, assigned to you, or that you seek to achieve. Feel free to make this list long and involved.

2. Several hours later or even the next day, revisit your list. Cross out those things that, on second reading, are not that crucial. Combine any items that appear similar to each other. The object of this second encounter is to dramatically pare down your list. If you have too many priorities, you are likely to feel anxious and frustrated.

3. Now, restructure, redefine, and rewrite your list if necessary. Keep seeking to streamline it. When in doubt, toss it out. If you're unsure if an item belongs on the list, chances are, it doesn't.

4. Put your list away and take it out the next day or the day after that. Now review it as if you are seeing it for the first time. Can any items be combined? Can anything be dropped? Should anything be reworded? As always, if something seems as if it is not that important, it probably isn't, so feel free to drop it!

5. Go ahead and make a working list of what you feel are your priorities at this time. Yes, things will shift and change as time marches on, but this is your list for now.

If it's helpful, use variations of the phrasing below in composing your choices:

> *"Achieve financial independence."*
> *"Strengthen my relationship with my spouse."*
> *"Provide for the education of my children."*

By wording your priorities in this way with an action expressed by a verb you are more inclined to take action than by simply jotting down "happy marriage," or "children's education."

As months and years pass, your priorities may shift. That's understandable. Since they are based on what you identify as important in your life, as it constantly changes, it makes sense that your priorities will change as well. For now, concentrate on the few important areas in your life as you have recently identified them.

Be sure to print your priorities on a small card that you can keep in your planner, purse, appointment book, or wallet. This affords you the opportunity to review your priorities periodically throughout the day, particularly when you are stuck in a line somewhere. It is all too easy to lose sight of the things we have deemed important in our rush-rush world. Simply reading your list of priorities on a regular basis is a powerful and reinforcing "self-organizing" technique.

Who says you can't move "getting organized" to the top of your priority list? Such a quest may not even be on your list at the moment. In the short term, however, it may make great sense to assign getting organized as a high priority.

You might be astonished by how much you can accomplish in a relatively short amount of time. What if you were to spend one day, one morning, or merely the next (solid) hour putting things in order? What if you treated the activity as if it had the utmost importance in your career or personal life? If you deemed getting organized to be of great importance, then, like other important things in your life, you would tend to it.

The structure of modern society virtually dictates that getting organized is one of the high priorities in your life, even if heretofore you haven't yet recognized it. To begin with, you need to be organized for reasons of safety. In nearly any environment, if there are things on the floor or items that are out of place, you can trip over them, bump into them, and find yourself in a hazardous situation.

Especially in the workplace, being organized translates into finding items more quickly and easily, being more responsive to others, and being more professional. Such characteristics contribute to the progression of your career and to your potential to receive raises and promotions. If you doubt the above, recall the messiest person in your workplace . . .

- Someone who routinely loses things
- Someone whose office is not a pleasure to visit
- Someone who is unreliable in returning borrowed items

Have you got that person in mind?

Q: How likely is that unorganized individual to be picked for a team when team members have the option of choosing?

Q: How likely is that person to receive a raise or promotion when there are others who are doing equally well and remain organized as they do their job?

You can see where this is heading! All things being equal, actively using and demonstrating organizational skills is one of the ever-present, if unarticulated, methods you can use to enhance your overall career prospects. Viewed in this light, it's relatively easy to make getting and staying organized a higher priority.

Establish Supporting Goals

NOW COMES THE PART WHERE YOU TAKE ACTION in support of those elements of your life you decided were important! Establish a variety of goal statements that correspond to each of the priority areas you have chosen. Seek to present these statements in positive terms, using positive terminology. If one of your priority areas is career success, and you have been the office clutter-bug for ten years, it will not help to set a goal such as, "I will not clutter my desk for one week."

What happens during that week? You begin to dwell on avoiding clutter day after day, hour after hour, until you become ineffective in doing your job. A more effective goal statement would be, "I will maintain a clear, clean desk this week."

Any goal worth pursuing will need to be:

❐ written   ❐ quantified   ❐ assigned a deadline

Writing your goals positively helps solidify your efforts. There is something about having your goals in a place where you can review them that makes them more real. At the very least, a visual reminder is a confirmation of their importance. At the most, they represent a formula guiding you to highly desirable end results.

"Quantified" means you attach a number. Say you want to receive an increase in salary of $4,000. The request is $4,000, not $3,975. If you happen to exceed your goal—well, lucky you!

A "deadline" means that you choose a specific target date (and time for goals of short duration) to complete what you set out to do. "The middle of the week" is vague. "Wednesday at 4:00 P.M." is specific. If you want to meet your deadlines, be specific!

Identifying priorities and establishing goals in support of those priorities is relatively simple compared to what comes next. Anybody can establish goals. Unfortunately, most people's goals are forgotten days or weeks after they first establish them. Reinforcing the goals that you set so that you actually achieve them requires something more than merely plans or words. Namely, it requires action!

Fortunately, there are many techniques that you can employ to see that you stick to the goals you set for yourself.

1.   Uniting with others, particularly with those who have goals in common with you, is a time-honored tradition. For example, someone who wishes to have more peace of mind might join a meditation group. Someone seeking to stay fit might look for a running partner. Those who want to read great books might seek to join or start a book club. Uniting with others could mean simply finding a friend who wants to achieve the same thing you do at the same time you do.

There is something about engaging in an activity with others that helps to ensure progress will continue. When you have no one to share the activity with, it is easy to slide. When someone is trying to achieve the same result as you, it's easier to have the support and encouragement from the friend, spouse, neighbor, relative, or whomever, than to have no one there to keep you motivated.

Suppose you tell me that you are going to accomplish X by next week. Then when we meet next week and I ask you about your goal, you'll either tell me that you accomplished it, or you'll tell me that you are somewhere close to achieving it, working on it, or haven't done anything about your goal at all. Simply knowing that we will be meeting and discussing your progress may be the driving force that you need to be successful.

2.   Visualize the completion of your goals; it's another powerful technique for increasing your probability of success. Many top athletes today visualize successfully completing the foul shot, catching the touchdown pass, hitting the home run, completing the triple axle jump, or clearing the hurdle, before actually doing so. By visualizing their performance, they increase the odds of a successful performance. Likewise, virtuoso pianists, ballet dancers, and professional speakers visualize successfully engaging in the task at hand before actually performing.

You can visualize successfully organizing your home, office, PC, desk, or any aspect of your work or life, and thereby increase the probability of succeeding. You probably visualize all the time, thinking about how it is going to be when you are with a loved one, having dinner that evening, or on vacation next spring. You can use the same process to see yourself becoming more organized.

Any goal, large or small, lends itself to the visualization process. Simply find a quiet place where you won't be disturbed, close your eyes, and let your imagination take hold. See yourself accomplishing exactly what you want to accomplish, in the way you want to accomplish it. See yourself as organized, in control, relaxed, and ready in ways that you know you can be.

3.   Surround yourself with reminders that you will constantly be exposed to. Using sticky pads or small notes, write out goal-reinforcing statements and post them on your mirror and in your appointment book, on the dashboard of your car, on or near your nightstand, on the refrigerator, by your front door, and wherever else you are likely to pass during the course of a day. Pleasantly surprise yourself!

Write something that is uplifting and supportive of your efforts like, "Today is going to be a great day for organizing my filing cabinet." Vary the statements so that you don't start to ignore them. Put them in creative places where you know you will encounter them and where they will have the most impact.

I like to leave a note to myself in my appointment book at the end of each day. Then, when I open up the appointment book to start the upcoming day, I see the uplifting note, routinely give myself a broad smile, and start working!

Stake Your Claim

TO REORDER THEIR LIVES ON A GRAND SCALE, some people devise an elaborate set of goals. It is the nature of a plan, however, not its complexity, that most affects its success. You are truly on the path to getting organized if your goal is a conscious and healthy one, a self-initiated choice; or however external the change may be, a more fundamental change has taken place internally.

When you lay claim to a goal, make the goal yours—you don't need outside stimulators. When you're willing to take responsibility for the outcome, a goal is indeed yours. A wonderful gauge for determining whether or not you are truly committed to your goal is to think about how you would feel if the goal were taken from you. Suppose you could no longer proceed down your chosen path, and all activity in pursuit of your goal had to cease.

- Would you be outraged?
- Would you object?
- Would you fight for your right to continue?

If you didn't achieve the goal, and you never laid claim to it, you could easily walk away from the task with no regrets. If you laid claim to a goal and didn't achieve it, you would have lingering feelings that you had failed yourself.

If a goal is not originally your creation, perhaps you have some leeway in the situations you encounter and can engage in shaping the goal. You may have to complete the entire store inventory, for example, by the end of the month. There are plenty of things you can do to make the task more enjoyable and rewarding for you, ultimately making it your own goal. Perhaps you can tackle the job one aisle at a time. Or, you may choose to begin with all of the high-priced items. By approaching an externally imposed task as a challenge, such as getting organized, it can be seen in a different light and internalized as your own goal.

When your mother used to tell you to clean your room, you probably did so begrudgingly, if you didn't adopt the goal as your own. Hers was an edict imposed from above that you "had to", although you disliked it. Sure, you were pleased with the results and would even have agreed that the room looked better and was more functional in an organized state. How much easier, however, would it have been all those times if you had adopted the goal of cleaning and organizing your room as if it were your own?

Today, the same solution potentially prevails. If you have been given the task of organizing financial records, the dining room table, or the patio, before getting started, take a few moments to contemplate the task:

- What will be involved?
- What kind of energy will you lend to the assignment?
- What will you do first?
- How will you take charge?
- How will you feel when the task is completed?

Can you personalize this task—make it your own? Of course you can! Even if it's a serial task to which you've been assigned, personalizing it makes it easier.

You'll find that your attitude changes once you've made the goal your own.

- Shovel the sidewalk in front of your house after the snowstorm? You bet, and when it's done, it's going to be the premier shoveling job in the neighborhood.
- Vacuum the rug in the living room? Of course! And the cleaner the rug is, the happier I am when I arrange my new furniture on it.
- Clean up that filthy workbench with its layers of dust, loose bolts and screws, and rusty old tools that you bought at a yard sale last summer and haven't touched since? Picture yourself as the guy who receives the admiration of everyone for the tool collection on your wall.

Part Three:

Listing and Charting Your Way

21

Recognize Fallibilities

AN ORGANIZATION MANAGEMENT PITFALL, particularly in recent years, is to rely on sophisticated scheduling tools as if they were the be all and end all. It makes sense to use palm top organizers, electronic calendars, time management software, day planners, and so on, if such tools:

- Support the way you live and work
- Are simple and convenient for you to use
- Are easy for you to keep current

A $100 bill says that you can't name a management tool that won't let you down the minute you don't keep the information it holds up to date. Recognize that all tools you use to manage your time, from simple to-do lists to complicated scheduling software, require continual input and updates. Otherwise, they quickly fail to reflect the current tasks and responsibilities you face. Even with voice recognition management and scheduling tools, you still have to "feed" the system.

With any planning or scheduling tool, someone has to be in the driver's seat. If you're not keeping up with the timelines you have established, particularly if you are relying on a scheduler in coordination with others, it will quickly become ineffectual. Likewise, if you bite off more than you can chew, planning and scheduling tools may alert you to what you have done, but it is up to you to get back on track and not rely on them too heavily. In that respect, the most critical factor in organizing, planning, and scheduling at all times is you! Ah, but you sensed that all along, didn't you?

Until sophisticated organization management tools come packed with a mechanical arm that literally moves the items accumulating on your desk, logs them in, and then ranks them based on your current task list and schedule, such tools will depend upon you, not vice versa. Until management mechanisms check your e-mail, fax machine, and voice mail, and assess and rank what each of those messages represent in terms of what you have to accomplish in the next hour, day, and week, half-heartedly using complicated technology will only put you out of sync.

Said most simply, your brain remains the most important tool in organizing your schedule, your time, and your life. The mental energy you bring to maintaining your organizing system is what fuels your efforts. Get some rest. A clear mind is a fundamental step on the path to a clear desk and an organized life.

Mark Your Calendar

DID YOU EVER STOP TO THINK that you can schedule some organizing tasks in your appointment book or calendar much as you would any other important obligation? If your desk is a semidisaster area, if you don't know what's in your overflowing drawers, and if you find yourself spending mounting minutes throughout the day hunting for crucial items, why not schedule some organizing time for later today or tomorrow?

Scheduling organizing time? Won't that represent another burden in a long line of tasks you face? Not so! Scheduling organizing time increases the probability that you will actually engage in essential organizing activities. It also reduces guilt. Many people feel as if maintenance tasks, such as getting organized and staying organized, intrude upon all the other "important" things scheduled in their day. If you fall into this camp, then you take your cue from others who have found that formally scheduling sessions for organizing automatically raises the task to the status of an important commitment.

The mere fact that you have scheduled a session on your calendar gives the job of organizing weight and a sense of importance that the task would not otherwise accrue. When Tuesday at 2:30 arrives, for example, and it's time for you to organize your second file drawer, you dutifully find yourself attending to the task much as you would any other item scheduled for that day. If you allot 45 minutes, then give your full attention to the task for that entire block of time. At the end of the 45-minute session, if you're not finished, you'll at least be much farther along than if you had never scheduled such a session!

If scheduling sessions sound pointless to you, go along with the suggestion anyway. Humor me. Schedule an organizing session on your calendar right now, and as the day and time approaches, give it your full attention and full resources, as you would any other item deemed worthy of being scheduled. You may be pleased, if not outright surprised, by the result.

Harnessing the power of deadlines in your schedule can also aid you in accomplishing objectives. Up until now, you may have dreaded deadlines and seen them as strictures imposed upon you that routinely foster stress and anxiety. However, deadlines can serve as powerful motivators toward the accomplishment of your goals. It all depends on the way you look at things!

I have written 32 books, but I wouldn't have finished book #1 if I tried to "write an entire book." Rather, my goal in approaching each book is to write one chapter at a time. Since most chapters are made of two or three subsections, I simply aim to finish one subsection, then another, then another until I finish a whole chapter. The rest of the day seems like a vacation.

The next day, I go back and start another chapter, approaching one subsection at a time. All the while, I acknowledge that I have a contract to honor and that a publisher is breathlessly waiting for my material. We pick a date in advance, and I agree to turn in the manuscript no later than that day.

Realistically, what do you think the chances are that I would turn in a manuscript on time if the publisher said over the phone, "Oh, we would like to have it in by the 21st or so"? The odds are that I would finish sometime after the 21st century. Having a contract that says on this date, the author will deliver the entire manuscript, dramatically increases the probability that I will finish the book in a timely fashion.

What deadlines do you face? Although your deadlines are probably imposed by external sources, you can turn them around with your newfound insight and use them to your advantage. (Hint: One of your deadlines comes around every April 15th. That's your favorite one, I'm sure.) What deadlines can you impose upon yourself to increase the probability of completing organizing goals that you have established in support of your priorities?

 23

Separate Long-Term and Short-Term Tasks

EVERYONE I KNOW IN THE WORKADAY WORLD (and a lot of people I don't know) use some kind of list as an organizing tool for getting things done. I'm neither for nor against any particular system you might use to stay efficient. Judge any system by your own personal results. However, if you haven't considered using what I call the super-long to-do list, give it a try.

If you already maintain some type of to-do list, you can use it more effectively to support your priorities by strategically lengthening it without overloading yourself. Your first super-long list will probably fill two to five pages. You'll have a clear idea of what you face all on one big roster, and you'll keep your priorities sharp for years to come. It doesn't have to follow a completely logical order at first; as you'll see momentarily, you can easily move items up to the front as needed. The front page contains tasks to accomplish in the short term.

The primary dilemma you're most likely to face is balancing the short-term against long-term tasks and activities. I have maintained a 10-page to-do list for years. I had hundreds of things on my to-do list, arranged according to my major life priorities. To keep from going crazy, I make sure most of the tasks on the list are medium- to long-range activities, and these do not appear on the first page.

In essence, I maintain a dynamic to-do list; it contains everything I want to get done, but always with only one page I need to look at: the top page. The first page of my list represents only the short-term activities—those I have chosen to do immediately or within a week. I draw continually from the 10-page list, moving items to the top as it becomes desirable or necessary to tackle them.

Yes, I am forever updating the list and printing out new versions, but there are so many advantages that I wouldn't think of doing it any other way, and you can't talk me out of it. I review the entire list periodically, always moving items from later pages up to the front page. Thus, anxiety stays at a rather low level.

Maintaining a long to-do list has helped me become more proficient in managing long-term or repeated tasks. Consider a situation where you have projects due, people waiting for your results, meetings to attend, and so forth. If I am working on a long-term project, I will continually draw to the front those portions that can be handled in the short-term. Likewise, if a task is a repeat or cyclical project—something I have to do every month or every year—I can move it up to the front page at the appropriate time without burdening myself by trying to constantly remind myself, "Oh yeah, in four and a half months, I definitely need to call that guy again and set up an appointment."

Most people who maintain some type of to-do list and tend to it on a daily basis allow their lists to carry over to the next day. Whatever they didn't finish on one day becomes part of the next day's to-do list. That's okay, but seek to finish today's tasks today.

Certain tasks, such as those that involve recurring organizational efforts, often receive short shrift when it comes to to-do lists. Don't shortchange yourself when listing recurring tasks.

In the hubbub of each day's activities, do you ever slip on to your to-do list stellar tasks such as:

- Organizing the magazine rack
- Clearing off the desk top
- Rearranging the supply cabinet

Such chores probably don't make your to-do list because they may not be vital, glamorous, or even remembered. Of course, when disorganization reaches a critical point and begins to cost you in terms of time, energy, or effort, it becomes an emergency. If a work or a leisure area gets so messy that you can't use it, the clutter begs for attention.

Listing organizing tasks on your to-do list before the situation develops into a mini-crisis helps you to stay in a "preventative" mode. This works well in other aspects of your life, so why wouldn't it work well here? For example, if you take your car in for a tune-up before you suspect a problem, you often spend far less money than if you had brought in your car after it had broken down, i.e., "Pay me now or pay me later." And you feel a lot better after taking your car for a "checkup" than you do after spending two hours walking to a gas station and then another two hours trying to find a tow truck in the middle of nowhere at 2:00 A.M.

Likewise, if you do things to maintain your health on a regular basis instead of waiting until you need a quadruple coronary bypass, you tend to live a longer, healthier life. Too many people short-change their health until after they've had a life or health-threatening wake-up call. When it comes to the continuing challenge of staying organized, listing some specific tasks on your to-do list will help you develop a "preventative maintenance" approach that will keep many organizing tasks from ever becoming large and unwieldy, and in the case of your kitchen, smelly and unpalatable.

On occasion you can short-circuit the to-do list and get stuff done without even entering it on your list. Most people who encounter information worth retaining and make a note of it, find that it may stay there for days, maybe months. To deal with incoming data faster, remember that useful information usually involves calling or writing to someone else.

Here's a way to skip several steps, cut down on the clutter, and notably increase your effectiveness on the job. Rather than adding a new task to your to-do list, try a fast-action option:

Pick up a pocket dictator or use voice recognition software to immediately dictate a letter or memo to whomever you need to contact about what it is you've come across, or dictate or type a message on your computer for immediate transmission by fax, e-mail, or Internet message.

Here's a little story about how I used a pocket dictator to bypass my to-do list. One fine Saturday morning, I was reviewing Peter Rich's section in *Readers' Digest*, where he reviews vocabulary words from books he's read. Years ago, I would have made a note to write to Mr. Rich and followed through on it sometime in the next six months or so. Instead, I grabbed my pocket dictator and created a letter to Mr. Rich stating which of my vocabulary words I thought his readers might enjoy. As soon as my transcriber typed the letter, I sent it. Thus, the item never made my to-do list.

How many times a day do you add to your to-do list when you could simply dictate a letter or memo, or type a message on your PC, and cut your overall time and effort by 75 percent?

24

Develop a Clarifying Checklist

CHECKLISTS ARE WONDERFUL, and, landsakes, you are already a master at producing checklists! ""Not me," you say? Well, what do you think a to-do list is? It's a crude checklist, often hastily composed with the items listed in no particular order. When it comes to getting organized, a few enhancements to the familiar to-do list will serve you well.

A checklist can have fewer than three items or more than nine items, but for practical purposes, a list usually works best within these limits. Too short and you don't exactly have a checklist. Too long and the list becomes overwhelming; you look at the list and think, "I'll never complete all this."

Pick one organizing task that needs immediate attention. To the best of your ability, create a to-do list (a checklist) of three to nine steps that will ensure your success of completing that one task. What will you need to do first? What will you have to do second?

As you compose your list, be gentle on yourself. The important issue is to first establish a plan. If you haven't worded it correctly or established the most logical sequence, do not fret.

Review and refine your list. Change the order of some tasks, combine some, elaborate upon, or divide up others. Ultimately, you will devise a sequence that represents a workable checklist, or you will devise a moronic sequence that leads to your doom.

Now, assuming your effort leads to the former and not the latter, honor your efforts by completing the checklist items as you listed them. Tackle the first task first and take it all the way to completion. If you can't proceed to completion, take it as far as you can, then go to task two, and so on.

Suppose your organizing challenge is to reclaim control of your dining room table. Here's what your checklist might look like:

1. Clear the entire table.
2. Dust and polish the table.
3. Clean the punch bowl or centerpiece.
4. Place it back in the center of the table.
5. Decide which of the other items belongs back in the punch bowl or around the centerpiece.
6. Clean and arrange the selected items.
7. Relocate, recycle, or discard items vanquished from the dining room table.
8. Invite someone to witness the results of your efforts! (In case you think no one will ever believe that you did it!)

When you receive praise for your efforts, the positive reinforcement increases the probability that you will extend your organizational efforts to other places within your home and office.

Maintain a Project List

You may be facing several organizing tasks in and around your office, home, and car, and within your desk, briefcase, wallet, or purse. Rather than attempt to tackle them all semiconcurrently, focus on one area at a time. If it helps, make one major clarifying list that cites each place or space in your life that you want to organize. On the other hand, you may not have enough paper for the number of lists you'll need . . .

The list could be ranked based on order of importance, estimated number of hours to completion, or degree of difficulty. Periodically review the list and pick the organizing tasks you've listed that you have the physical, mental, and emotional strength to initiate. Once you begin on the selected task, strive fervently for completion—proceed all the way to the end of what it takes for you to be fully organized in this area.

Alternatively, if the task is large or multifaceted, such as rearranging your four-drawer filing cabinet at work, combine your efforts with the advice from tips #10, Reward Thyself and #60, Divide, Literally, and Conquer.

Keep the list in a handy place, where you can find it easily and peruse it often. Having the list handy is more important than you might think. Today, we are all confronted by the many items that "compete" for our time and attention—it's relatively easy to lose sight of what we want to accomplish. Everything gets churned up in the daily grind of having too much to do. The simple act of preparing a clarifying list of organizing projects and periodically examining the list can help you enormously.

25

Map It Out

FOR SOME PEOPLE, preparing an outline of what needs to be done is drudgery, whereas a visual plotting, sometimes called a mind map, is less onerous, and dare I say it, even fun. If you're a visually oriented person, you may find relief in mapping out your organizational quest. Take any particular organizing task that you face and, to the best of your ability, describe the task in a brief, simple phrase. Write that phrase in the center of a piece of paper and circle it.

Then, from the circle outward, draw a line with an arrow at the end of it to the first thing that comes to mind. For example, if you are a high school student seeking to get into college and you haven't started your application process, the organizing task that you write in the middle of your page might be, "get into college." The first line with an arrow might point to a second phrase such as, "list my top ten school choices."

From there, you might have anywhere from three to ten choices, each of which could merit its own arrow. If it helps, write the name of each possible college at the end of an arrow. Returning to your central task (in the middle of the page), contemplate your first move in organizing your "get into college" campaign. You may require the mail and e-mail addresses of each of the institutions. So, draw another line with an arrow and write, "acquire contact data."

Another line extending from your central task might read, "obtain application materials." Since most institutions have some type of downloadable application form available via their Web site, you might not have to spend a dime on postage.

As a corollary to obtaining the application forms, you might also want to acquire the respective university brochures, orientation kits, or course catalogs. You might wish to receive hard copies of these items or download them from the Web. Either way, additional lines with additional arrows should point to these adjacent tasks.

Some people find it helpful to use colored pens or highlighters to stimulate creativity and make the page more visually pleasing. The key is to let the "sparks fly" as you create your visual map. You don't have to answer to anyone in the process. If you want to use boxes, little squares, stars, or any other symbol, it's up to you. If you want to connect tasks by broken lines, dotted lines, double lines, or squiggly lines, you're in charge!

Soon your page will start to fill. Beginning in the center and branching out in many different directions, you create a visual map of the key activities and tasks involved in organizing and executing your "get into college" campaign. Likewise, you could use a single sheet of paper to map out other organizational challenges. When your map is complete, or mostly done, start using it as your trail guide. Execute the tasks as you plotted them on the special page. (Also see the tips to chart your path in tip #36.)

Chart Your Path

PALM-TOP COMPUTERS ENABLE YOU TO TAKE YOUR PLANS with you as you travel, maintain your database of contacts, send faxes, keep up with e-mail, and log onto the Internet, from anywhere in the world. With the accelerating pace of new technology, more new tools are available than ever before for helping you stay organized. Several varieties of organizing and planning software are on the market, and enable you to:

- Manage your daily, weekly, and monthly schedules
- Align your daily activities with important and urgent tasks you face
- Engage in project planning
- Share files via downloads
- Electronically link your plans and schedules with others

The underlying components of effectively organizing your day while making progress on selected tasks and projects remain the same. Any goal that you intend to achieve needs to be written down, quantified, and assigned a specific time frame. If you don't have a timeline attached to a task or project, then "any time" will do, and "never" is the likely result. Never is a long time.

More powerful, more feature-laden scheduling software, calendar systems, and other project organizers become available with each passing month. Most of these support tools offer some highly convenient common elements, including the following:

- A calendar system for keeping and tracking appointments, identifying schedule conflicts, and flagging areas and times of critical activity
- A variety of chart forms, including milestone charts, flow charts, and calendars
- Drop-down menus, drag-and-drop techniques, and convenient icons
- The flexibility to add or subtract activities in any desired sequence
- Colors, symbols, and other tools that offer at-a-glance viewing

- Alarms and buzzers that toggle on and off, set at times and intervals at your whim
- The ability to fax, e-mail, or download any chart file onto a Web site
- Multiple options for printing any chart

No matter how sophisticated the task or scheduling software you may be employing, it will be of little use if the information you are adding is not current or is inaccurate (see tip #21). Garbage in yields garbage out, with scheduling and organizing tools, nothing in yields nothing out!

Whether you use more sophisticated project management and scheduling software on your computer or palm-top, or you use traditional nontechnical types of tools, such as hand-drawn charts or grids, carefully plotting your steps will lead to these highly desirable results:

- Significant increase in your probability of accomplishment
- Greater productivity
- Effective time management

The three basic forms of project management and/or scheduling tools are milestone charts, flow charts, and calendars. These tools are briefly discussed in the following tips.

27

Plot Your Way

A MILESTONE CHART, formally known as a Gantt chart after origi-
nator Henry L. Gantt, is probably familiar to you (but you had no
idea it was called a Gantt chart). Depicted below, it offers you a
quick view of your progress on a variety of tasks and projects in
relation to time:

	Month 1	Month 2	Month 3	Month 4	Month 5
Task 1	>>>>>>	>>>>>>>>	>>>		
Task 2		>|>>>>>>>>	>>>>>>>>	>>>>>	
Task 3			>>>>>>	>>>>>>>	
Task 4				>>>>>>>>	>>

Here is how it works: Suppose one of your priorities is to
advance in your career. One of your goals in support of that priority is to achieve a raise of $6,324 at the next quarterly perfor-
mance and appraisal session, scheduled in 11 weeks. To reach that

goal, you've identified five tasks that will greatly enhance the value of your services to your boss and the higher-ups in your division. These tasks include:

- Rewriting the orientation manual for new hires
- Getting an article published in one of the top three magazines in your industry
- Starting an online monthly newsletter for your firm's top clients and prospects
- Completing the report three weeks before it is due
- Participating at the key trade show by making important contacts, and gathering critical information for your boss

Adding these five accomplishments to your performance record over the next 11 weeks, along with what you already do in the normal course of the day and week, will be challenging; but hey, you're a trooper. Your mission now becomes to allocate your time and resources to complete each of the tasks with a flourish, and to position yourself for the salary increase you're after.

A more sophisticated visual tool is to plot each of the activities on the milestone chart so that you have a clear indication of both the timeline and sequencing of each of these activities, and how they will support your overall goal.

To begin, plot the most basic information for each project. Then, extending the process a bit further, add subtasks under each task area. For example, to get the article published, you may first have to interview some people or conduct some research. These could be depicted as subtasks. You might have to organize your notes, create an outline, then write a first draft, then possibly a second draft, and have a colleague review the article before you submit a final draft. Finally, you will be able to submit a final draft to publishers.

Item \ Task	1	2	3	4	5	6	7	8	9	10	11
Rewrite manual	>>	>>>>>	>>>>>	>>							
Publish article		>>>	>>			>>>>		>>>			
Online zine					>>>	>>>>>	>>>>>	>>>>>	>>>>>	>>>>>	
DEF report						>>	>>>>>	>>>			
Trade show							>>>	>			

28

Add Subtasks to Your Chart

DEPENDING ON HOW MUCH DETAIL YOU NEED or can stand, you may have anywhere from six to ten subtasks in support of a given task. How much detail you choose to portray in the chart is your choice. The important thing is that what you record is of value to you—it helps you continue your progress toward your chosen goals.

With the other tasks, you may find yourself plotting anywhere from two or three subtasks to fifteen or more.

Continuing with the example of arranging to get an article published, you would want to list the level of detail that serves you. If you complicate the chart, it could be counterproductive to your purposes. To enhance your chart, add symbols such as a broken line, which can denote germination, or put footnotes at the bottom of the chart; place left and right arrows, which can indicate distinct periods of activity, and insert blanks that indicate no activity!

You can write people's initials next to particular subtasks. Then you can easily see whose cooperation is needed or to whom you will delegate the entire subtask. For example, in writing an article, maybe you will charge one person with gathering all the research information before handing it off to you.

You can also use colors to help guide you along, whether the chart is on the wall, on a single piece of paper in a file folder, or on your hard drive. Green, for example, could be used to denote the start of tasks. Yellow could indicate some critical function. Blue could represent completion. Depending on the level of detail with which you are comfortable, you could devise separate milestone charts for each task.

If you're working with different people on each task, then a separate milestone chart might make it easier for them. Similarly, when you consider the broad range of priority areas in your life and the goals you've adopted in support of them, multiple milestone charts may seem preferable. Still, you want to keep things as simple as possible, otherwise, you'll need help organizing your organizing charts.

Item	1	2	3	4	5	6	7	8	9	10	11
Rewrite manual	>>	>>>>>	>>>>>	>>							
Publish article		>>	>>>>>	>>>>>	>>>>>	>>>>>	>>>>>	>>>>>	>>>>>	>>>>>	>
Interviews		>>									
Research		>>									
Organize			>								
Outline				>>							
1st draft						>>					
Peer Review						>>					
2nd draft							>>				
Submit								>			
Follow up											>
Online zine				>>>	>>>>>	>>>>>	>>>>>	>>>>>	>>>>>		
DEF report					>>	>>>>>	>>>				
Trade show							>>>	>			

29

Organize with Flow Charts

MOST PEOPLE HAVE HAD EXPERIENCE WITH FLOW CHARTS at one time or another, and for most, it was not traumatic. Perhaps you remember an instance when one of your teachers in grade school drew a square, then drew a line to another square or circle, then down to yet another object. It could have been your math teacher depicting the relationship between numbers, your history teacher explaining the convoluted migration of nomadic peoples, your science teacher illuminating the interaction of chemical compounds, or your physical education teacher trying desperately to explain the game of kickball.

While flow charts are widely used to convey a process (how something happens), they are also quite convenient for helping you to:

- Track project progress
- Stay on target
- Accomplish your goals and stay organized

Flow charts can extend downward or to the right. In business, they usually extend to the right so that a timeline can be added to the top or bottom of the chart.

Flow charts are particularly useful in plotting activities related to a task or project area where many different people or resources may be required, and where contingencies come into play. You can look at several possible outcomes with such a chart. If the answer to a question is yes, the flow chart proceeds along one path, and if the answer is no, it proceeds along another. Flow charts also allow for feedback loops. If an article is submitted to a publication and the editor wants specific changes, the feedback loop could encompass where you go next. You can also buy erasable charts—a valuable feature for making course corrections.

As with milestone charts, you can use colors and symbols to convey different types of information at a glance. If you add a key at the bottom of the chart that shows exactly what each symbol and color represents, then you can't go wrong.

Track Your Progress

USING A CALENDAR TO ENSURE PROGRESS TOWARD chosen goals is a time-honored method of staying organized. Suppose one of your projects will be initiated and completed in the same calendar month. You are going to prepare a completely new orientation manual for new hires. As the illustration below indicates, the due date is March 31st. So, on March 31st you write, "complete manual."

To make this system work, use actual calendar pages from the current year for however many months are relevant to the project you are managing. If you haven't yet organized your desk, you may want to post the calendar pages on the wall to avoid losing them. Working from that end date back to the present, what needs to take place right before you deliver the new orientation manual?

If eight working days prior to the deadline (the 22nd), you need to meet with some department heads to offer your briefing and obtain their input, then you schedule a conference on that day.

MARCH						
Sunday	Monday	Tuesday	Wednesday	Thursday	Friday	Saturday
	1	2	3	4	5	6
7	8	9 Initiate review	10	11	12	13
14	15 Proofread manual	16	17	18	19 Assemble copies	20
21	22 Schedule conference	23	24	25	26	27
28	29	30	31 Complete manual			

Likewise, you determine what needs to happen before the conference, as well as what comes directly after. In each case, plot the dates on the calendar, then you could connect them with lines or arrows that show the relationships of the dates. As in the case of milestone charts and flow charts, you may use colors and symbols to give you a quick visual review of your progress.

With this calendar "Block-back" method, you can quickly see that if you miss any interim dates on the calendar in pursuit of successful completion of the project, then finishing subtasks at all other interim dates becomes jeopardized. Each interim date represents a mini-deadline. Hence, you have a built-in system for ensuring that your project will continue according to plan.

For goals that stretch on for years or decades, starting with the end in mind is the only practical way to proceed. Milestone charts, flow charts, and large wall calendars are available at office supply stores and at the respective Web sites of these companies. So, go shopping!

Part Four:

Reclaiming Your Places and Spaces

31

Start from Scratch

WHEN YOU HAVE A PLACE OR SPACE that you wish to organize, particularly if a little straightening up is long overdue, it often makes sense to clear the area completely before you proceed. Consider the case of your car's glove compartment, please! The typical glove compartment might contain maps, an owner's manual, car registration materials, pens, pencils, paper, pennies, newspaper clippings, discount tickets to restaurants, and supermarket coupons.

How are you going to deal with such a mess? Empty the whole compartment and put everything on the seat next to you. As you wade through the accumulation, throw out the gum wrappers and other debris. Check the expiration dates on coupons, and chuck any that have expired. Keep the rest bound by a rubber band or paper clip.

Take the maps, car registration materials, and any other important documents, and lay them flat on the bottom of the glove compartment where they occupy the least space. Put back any items you deem essential such as tissues, pens and pencils, and other items that can lay reasonably flat. Put the discount coupons in last since those are items you'll want to review periodically.

Larger items that you want to keep in the glove compartment, such as a camera, medication, a hat, or gloves (hey, some people keep gloves in the glove compartment) go in last because they can rest comfortably on the aforementioned items.

Clearing out the glove compartment is easier than trying to organize it by sticking a hand or two deep into the mess and attempting to jostle things around. When everything is temporarily extracted, it becomes evident which items need not be replaced. You also have a better opportunity to re-evaluate the need for long-standing items contained in your glove compartment. If you have four maps, but you've only used one in the last nine months, maybe the other three can go in a valise in the trunk. Also, there may be items in your glove compartment stashed there years ago that you've never used. Upon review, you could decide that the car is not the best place to store them.

You might conclude that other items not previously kept in the glove compartment ought to be. In the storage space's newly organized state, there will be room for such items—until you let the glove compartment become totally disorganized again. (Just kidding; I know you're not going to let that happen anymore.)

Use a "pay as you go" system—no ad hoc outposts, no accumulations, and no piles. Once you develop the habit of clearing space in all the compartments of your life: your car, closets, medicine cabinets, etc., you accomplish many things. You demonstrate to yourself that you actually have the ability to stay organized, manage your affairs, and conduct your life; you remain in a ready state to handle what comes next rather than trying to merely squeak by!

Pretend it's Day One—When your places and spaces become too disorganized, pretend that it is "day one" and rearrange the area from scratch. This highly viable strategy works particularly well with your desktop. Think back, for example, to when you assumed your current position at work. On day one, when you approached your office, cubicle, or other workspace, in what condition was the room, your desk, any nearby filing cabinets, closets, and other spaces? You guessed it: empty. Imagine you're sitting down at your desk for the first time. Would you continue to include the items currently on it and would you place them in their current locations? If so, feel free to leave them where they are.

Reconsider the particulars of how you work with the materials in your office. Should some items be moved to the right or left? Should anything be removed from the desktop? Does something need to be added? Consider every instance when you reach across the desk unnecessarily. If you're right-handed, consider the times that you reach across to the left side for something. Can you rearrange all of your tools for economy of motion so that you do less maneuvering? Alternatively, are there items you prefer to have more than an arm's length away so that you will stretch throughout the course of a day? Whatever you decide, the configuration of your desktop has to uniquely suit the way you work and operate. Never mind what somebody else down the hall is doing! Adopt the "day one" mindset, and you may discover a desk and workspace arrangement that is novel for you, representing a boost in productivity and enjoyment.

32

Conquer Your Desk

FOR THE PURPOSE OF STAYING ORGANIZED, as well as managing your time and feeling energized, clear your desk and surrounding area each evening as you end work for the day. Yes, you read it correctly—every evening before you depart. This will also help you start out at your best the next day.

I've discussed the issue of getting organized with top achievers in many different professions including corporate executives, airline pilots, plant managers, even fellow authors and speakers! Each and every person I questioned agrees that when his or her desk or office and personal surroundings are in order, he or she feels far more energized at the start of the day. Conversely, when these top achievers come into their offices at the start of the day and see a huge mess, they feel somewhat defeated.

Clearing your desk and surroundings each evening requires discipline. Most people don't want to clear their desks. It's a whole lot easier just to depart for the day. However, when you arrange your materials in the evening for higher productivity the next morning, a host of benefits come into play. When you leave with a clear desk, you give yourself a sense of closure or completion to your day.

When you arrive in the morning and find yourself greeted by clear, clean surroundings, you gain a psychological boost. What's more, you're either automatically drawn to the most important leftover issue, or you get to make a fresh decision about what materials to extract from your desk, filing cabinet, or shelves based on what you want to accomplish that morning. This is often more productive than merely dealing with what you left on the desk the night before.

Some projects span several days, and for that reason, it can be prudent on occasion to leave one (and only one!) file folder open on your desk so that it will catch your attention first thing the next morning. However, you don't want to fall into the habit of leaving unfinished piles on your desk each night. If you have one project, one file folder, or one of whatever you're working on in front of you, and the rest of your desk is clutter free, you are going to have:

- More energy
- More focus
- More direction
- More motivation

Consider the top of your desk, even if you can no longer see it through all the unkempt piles. What, precisely, do you need to have on it? A quick answer is: anything you use on a recurring and daily basis. This could include a pen, a roll of tape, a stapler, a staple remover, Post-It pads, a ruler, paper clips, and so on. Anything that you can't use on a daily or recurring basis does not belong on your desktop. Such items are best stored in a drawer within your desk, or possibly on a table or credenza behind you.

Why bother to make the distinction between what you use on a daily or recurring basis versus what you don't? Because, your goal at all times is to have as much open space as possible to support the way you work. You want clear, clean, flat surfaces. You literally need a disembarking area—a place where you can open packages and break down the mail, thereby diminishing piles and accumulations.

Examples of Useful Items for Your Desk
- Paper
- Letterhead
- Business envelopes
- Letter opener
- Stamps
- Ruler
- Stapler and staple remover
- Scissors
- Business cards
- Drawer dividers
- Tissues
- Pens, pencils, highlighters, and felt-tip pens
- Markers
- Note cards and greeting notes
- Scratch paper and Post-It pads
- Paper clips

Place supporting and familiar items near your desk, but not on it. This includes personal objects, such as pictures, plants, and personal motivators. Also, if an item enhances your productivity, efficiency, and creativity, place it near, but not on, your desk. Okay, maybe you can keep a few small, personal items on your desk, such as pictures or toys.

Useful Tools for Surrounding Areas
- Filing folders
- Large wastebasket
- Bulletin board

These are tools that you will need on hand when you are mailing, filing, and engaging in other routine office chores. Long-life stamps, which can be printed with "Draft" or "Review and Return" can cut down on the time you spend writing by hand when organizing and sending out materials.

Hereafter, manage your desktop as if it's one of the most important elements to staying organized, because it is. Recognize that when you begin each morning with a clear, organized desk and a clean, organized office, you work with more energy, focus, direction, and motivation. It becomes easier to concentrate on the tasks that you deem most important and urgent.

What's Inside Counts

Inside your desk you want to retain items that you use on a weekly basis, although items used daily can be stored there, too. Recognize, however, that your desk drawers are not for storing supplies. You may store a pad of paper, but not pads of paper. You only need one pad at a time; you're not opening your own office supply store. The general principle is to have an item there if and when you need it. Keep pads of paper and other extra supplies in a file folder, a storage locker, or in some other space away from the epicenter of your creative and productive post.

If you choose to use one of your desk drawers to contain file folders, then obviously it would house file folders of highly current projects. Put the important and urgent materials at the front and the least important and least urgent materials at the back. Files are most useful when there are only important documents inside. Routinely discard extraneous information, and be on the lookout for opportunities to reduce, shrink, and pare down the piles. Retain only the materials that are essential.

Once you have only those things on your desktop that ought to be on your desktop, and only those things in your desk that ought to be in your desk, then proceed to the other storage compartments around your office. You can do it!

Make Your Shelves Work for You

YOU PROBABLY HAVE SOME TYPE OF SHELVING IN YOUR OFFICE, cubicle, or work area. The question of what to house on your shelves versus what is best contained in a filing cabinet is relatively easy to answer. Essentially, shelves are best used to do the following:

- Temporarily store items you are bound to use within 10 to 15 days
- Store items that are too large to go in a filing cabinet
- Present a collection of like items, such as 12 issues of the same magazine, in an upright magazine storage box
- House projects in progress

- Store books, directories, supply catalogs, and other items with spine labels

Remember that items you are temporarily storing on shelves are ideally used in 10 to 15 days; they don't hang around for 40 to 60 or more days. It's exceedingly easy to lose track of this. Once a temporary pile becomes a permanent file, you begin to lose control of what you're retaining. Clutter in your office starts to mount, and you wonder again why you feel so disorganized!

Be careful as well when storing elements of a project in progress on your shelves. It's fine to temporarily park the brunt of materials you are working with so that you can have a few materials before you at any given time. However, if you're maintaining an orderly desk, then the project materials at hand should rotate from your desk to the shelf and back to your desk. The mass of materials needs to get thinner in the process, and eventually not appear on your shelves at all.

The Lighter the Load, the Better

As more and more stuff floods into your office, you'll find it's no feat to fill up your shelves in record time. All the office supply catalogs, annual directories, software instruction guides, and company policy and procedure manuals contribute to quickly turn an open space into a "no vacancy" situation. This is why it is crucial to keep supplies in an actual supply cabinet.

Supply cabinets are designed to house items in bulk. These items might be stacked on top of one another, placed horizontally, or end to end. Ideally, your supply cabinet is farther away from your desk than your shelves. While you want to strive to arrange items on your shelves with precision, supply cabinets allow for a lot more leeway.

The benefit of using supply cabinets is that you are able to simply open them and readily find what you need. It helps if you keep like items together. However, extreme neatness is only marginally important here. The bigger the office staff sharing the same supply cabinet, the more important neatness becomes. (So, once again, neatness counts, like your third-grade teacher used to say.) If you're in a small office, as long as all employees can find what they need within the supply cabinet, it is probably okay.

Interconnectedness

Organized individuals eventually grasp that the relationship between one's desk, shelves, and supply cabinet is not static. What is housed in one location ultimately may be housed somewhere else, depending on the following:

*   The tasks at hand
*   The available resources to meet those tasks
*   The time frame

Always be on the prowl for what can be tossed or recycled. If you don't need it, it's probably not worth filing or storing. Too many people feel fearful about tossing items because they simply know they will "need it the next day." "I know the moment I toss something . . ." Actually, this is not nearly as great a problem as one might imagine in the information age.

Almost any list, report, or document that you can name can be replaced. Somebody else has a copy; it's on the Internet; or it's on somebody's hard drive. If you can't think of a good reason to hang onto something, then that is a good reason to toss it. Many executives retain information at work only to tuck it away, never to be used again. Even if the professionals are off by 25 to 50 percent in their estimates, it still means that much of what you are hanging on to could be deadwood. The more you clear out your office, the easier it is to find the important things that you've retained.

Win the Paper Chase

MILT KNEW THAT HE NEEDED TO GET ORGANIZED, but he let years pass without addressing the issue. He would do anything but straighten his files. Yet, when he needed to find something, he spent untold hours rummaging around and was never in control. Milt could not be trusted to return anything. This reputation hampered his career and working relationships. It probably restricted his earnings . . . need I say more?

Knowing where to find things, such as necessary papers, files, and other documents is a sign of competence and provides freedom to concentrate on creative, fulfilling work, and not the clutter that surrounds you. Unfortunately, most career professionals today are plagued by more paper than their predecessors of a generation ago, despite the long-standing promise that we'd all be working in "paperless offices." If you analyzed your most repetitive task, chances are that handling paper would top the list on most days. In many respects, getting organized is synonymous with paper handling!

There's little wonder that it's so easy to become disorganized in record time considering the volume of paper everyone handles daily. Figures from the U.S. Postal Service reveal that last year more than 20 billion catalogs were mailed in the U.S.—that's the equivalent of 70 catalogs for every man, woman, and child in America. If you retain all of those catalogs, no wonder you're buried in paper!

Despite the popularity of e-mail, the Direct Marketing Association reports that the growth rate in the total volume of regular, third-class, bulk mail (fondly known as junk mail) continues to increase at a pace faster than growth rate in the population. The U.S. Postal Service shows that the typical executive receives more than 225 pieces of unsolicited mail each month. I've calculated that the average person spends a total of eight solid months of his or her life reading junk mail. Greenpeace, an organization dedicated to protecting the environment, annually sends out 25,000,000 pieces of direct mail to its huge database of members, supporters, and prospects.

Your mission is to whittle down all those pages of catalogs, magazines, and other voluminous materials that come your way so that you deal with only what you need. You can avoid being besieged with paper by reducing the potential for disorganization from the start, such as the moment when:

- You receive the daily mail
- Somebody hands you something
- Something happens to fall into your inbox

Use your copier as often as possible to retain the few pages you need from a book or other item. Scan key paragraphs and pages directly onto your hard drive, where it will be easily searchable and retrievable via your various word processing functions. This is superior to filing something and then trying to find it on your own. A word of caution: Don't make the mistake of overscanning, or you'll fill up your hard drive as quickly as you filled up your filing cabinets. Disorganization, either electronic or manual, is equally anxiety provoking.

Use a junk drawer as a holding bin when stuff comes to you too quickly, such as when you're in the middle of an important project, or when you simply "can't deal with that right now." Later, when you have an opportunity, go to your junk drawer, and plow through it as much as you can. Then, use this four-step process for assessing where the items will go:

1. Act on it
2. Delegate it
3. File it
4. Recycle or toss it

Rank the items in your thin "act on it" file according to what is important and urgent, moving down to what is unimportant and not urgent. Understandably, this category ought to always be the smallest.

Questions That Count

If it helps, ask yourself a series of questions that can help you quickly determine what to do with the next item that crosses your desk. These include questions such as:

- What does this document represent?
- Is there any reason to retain this?
- Who else needs to know about this?

If an item you receive merits your attention and actually requires you to get back in touch with someone, use the path of least resistance to resolve the issue. In other words, use, if you can:

- Fax instead of mail
- E-mail instead of fax
- Pay by credit card instead of by check
- Call instead of visit

Continually Be on the Lookout

Throughout the day, when the spirit moves you, examine your desktop, desk drawers, shelves, filing cabinet, and storage cabinet to determine what, if anything, no longer needs to be retained. This includes outdated directories or instruction manuals you know you're not going to use again. Also identify any outdated flyers, annual reports, PR materials, announcements, catalogs, and invitations. Gentle hint: If you don't find anything, go back and search for real!

Feel free to chuck old editions of books that you'll never open again. You can also throw away back issues of magazines that you haven't touched for more than a year or two. Toss bottles of whiteout that have more than dried solid. Get rid of scraps, rough drafts, memos, correspondence, reports, and any documents that do not have to be retained. Chuck the excess vendor supply catalogs that you may have on hand, as well as duplicate items, annual reports that you don't look at, software you received in the mail that you are never going to explore, and take-out restaurant menus from places you never go to.

Face Files with Smiles

FILING IS THE ULTIMATE ORGANIZATIONAL TECHNIQUE, which is unwelcome news to some. When you file items intelligently, you enable yourself to efficiently withdraw what you need when you need it. As Jim Cathcart, author of *The Acorn Principles,* says, "Filing is not about storing, it is about retrieval." You file things because either they will help you to be prosperous in the future (the information you retain has power), or because there are penalties for not filing (you won't be able to complete your taxes). All items that you file should have potential future value. When it comes to organizing files, the popular choice is to park them in a filing cabinet—preferably one with doors that open and close rather easily. Since most of the files that you maintain at home are not legal size, the standard width filing cabinet will do fine. There are many varieties at office supply stores, including one drawer, two drawers, etc., up to five drawers.

Start with a two-drawer filing cabinet that is about 18 to 24 inches in length. You probably won't need anything larger. Use colored file folders to separate items so as to give you visual control of your drawer.

Think of the last time you were in your doctor's office. If the doctor's patient files were exposed, chances are you saw some kind of color-coded filing system. This kind of system enables the office staff to go right to the appropriate area, which cuts down on the time spent searching for any particular file. Color-coded files help you find things more quickly and easily. You could assign green file folders for anything that has to do with, say, money, blue for anything that has to do with your career progression, yellow for anything related to taxes, and so on.

Desk drawers can also serve as filing cabinets, although the space is limited. Unless the desk is well designed, it is often difficult to easily open and close the drawer. Storing the information that you file and extract on a regular basis nearby is convenient, and I recommend it.

If you find that the files are becoming voluminous, with little slack in the drawers, first prune what you can. Chuck old and obsolete papers, duplicates, and anything else you feel that you don't need to retain. That exercise alone may enable you to avoid buying a one- or two-drawer filing cabinet. The moment you have to stuff files to force them into the drawer, and pull with considerable tug to extract them, it's a reasonable bet that there is a filing cabinet in your future. As long as you have about 20 percent of your desk drawer vacant, you're in decent shape.

If it's been about a half millennium since you organized your filing cabinet, rather than attempt to redo the whole thing, tackle only half a drawer every week. This will keep you at a safe and sane pace. Assemble the tools you'll need to be effective, such as several blank file folders, file folder labels, magic markers, and anything else that supports your efforts. You may also need to use color-coded dots, a stapler, paper clips, fasteners, sticky pads, and other organizing tools. Rather than using two or three manila folders, feel free to splurge——buy black, green, pink, orange, or blue folders.

Simply grab the first file in the drawer you have chosen to tackle. Examine its contents.

- What can be combined?
- What needs to be reallocated?
- What color folder or what color label will you use to house the remaining materials?

Everything in the file is subject to being combined, deleted, or moved around. Your goal at all times is to ensure that the things you have chosen to file are housed in their best possible location.

Go into the second file in the drawer and similarly whip through it and allocate its contents. If you're not sure that something is worth retaining, chances are it's not worth retaining, since most of us have a tendency to overretain and overfile. Chances are astronomically high that you can safely pare down a large portion of your files and suffer no consequences whatsoever. As always, the less you have, the easier it is to find that which you chose to retain.

When you have gone through your half-drawer, relax, give yourself a break, and go do something else. You don't have to tackle the second half of the drawer until a week or so from now.

Fewer Files, More in Them

Always seek to have fewer large files of like items as opposed to a larger number of smaller files. Why? You'll find it far easier to extract what you are looking for if you only have to deal with a few large files to begin with. You will find the right file with ease, since there are only a few choices. It will then take you time to go through that file to find the particular document, but your odds of success will be high because you have already confined your search to a specific area.

Conversely, if you have dozens and dozens of small files, you might not extract the correct file even after three or four tries. If you are lucky, and you do extract the correct file, the time required to find the desired page within the file won't be that much less than if you had pulled the desired page from a larger file.

Some people swear by date stamping. Every time something goes into your file, you stamp the corner of it indicating on what day it was placed in the file. If you're comfortable with doing this, go ahead. However, there aren't really any negative consequences to not stamping. Usually, an item's importance is not related to the date on which you filed it, although the longer an item has lingered in your files without ever being used, the higher the probability that you can safely chuck it.

What you file and how you file is largely governed by the file headings—the labels you place on the tab section of each file folder. It is easy enough to label one file folder "Office Supplies," and another "Personal Documents," but you want to be creative in your labeling to accommodate the gaggle of stuff that comes your way. You'll probably find that some of the influx doesn't seem to have a proper home. Who is to say that you cannot label your file folders with the following?

- Review this after the first of the year
- Hold until after the merger
- Check in one month
- Review next spring
- Don't know where to file

By having a file labeled "Don't Know Where to File", you auto-matically create a home for the handful of things that your instincts tell you to retain, but which simply don't fit anything else that you're doing. Now, at least you have a fair chance of getting your hands back on such items when, low and behold, the time might be right to reread them closely.

Don't worry that a file labeled "Don't Know Where to File" may grow too large too quickly. You always have the opportunity to open that file quickly, review its contents, and make decisions regarding what you see—acting, delegating, re-filing, or tossing it. When you review a re-filed item a second or third time, you can almost auto-matically toss it. So, get your wastebasket ready.

Establish Rotating Tickler Files

THERE ARE EXTREME BENEFITS TO SETTING UP a daily and monthly "rotating tickler file." Suppose something crosses your desk in March—it looks interesting, but you don't have to act on it until April 25th. If you have one file folder for each month of the year, January to December, you can park the item in the April folder.

Going further, you could set up an additional 31 file folders marked #1 through #31. Now, when April comes around, you open up the April file folder, take out all the contents, and allocate the items to file folders #1 through #31 as appropriate. You stick the April file folder at the end of the pack, so that the month of May is now in front, preceded by the file folders for the individual days of the current month.

These 43 file folders, #1 through #31 and January through December, allow you to park anything in the appropriate place when the item doesn't have to be dealt with too soon. If you receive something on the 3rd day of the month, but you don't have to deal with it until the 18th, put it in the folder marked the 18th, or better yet, to give yourself some slack, put it in a folder two or three days before the 18th.

When you institute tickler files, much of the clutter and stuff on your desk and around your office will immediately gain a home, because you've set a date when you're going to review the materials. They are off your desk, off your counters, and off your mind. Yet, you haven't lost them. You have simply placed them in a location where you'll be able to retrieve them at a time when it makes the most sense to deal with them.

You can use a tickler file to write out your checks and pay your bills, and then store the envelopes in the appropriate folder prior to sending. Many people who use tickler files find it convenient to review them at the start of each week, and perhaps one or two more times during that week. One of the benefits of this system is that when you review an item days, weeks, or months after first putting it in the tickler file, you often have a greater sense of objectivity. Choosing to act on it, delegate it, re-file it, or toss it becomes easier. Happily, much of what you review gets tossed. Thus, you'll find less clutter, greater organization, and greater focus and direction in terms of the pressing tasks that you face. Isn't that why you're here?

Creating Files in Advance of the Need

A variation on the theme of employing both file labels and using tickler files is creating files in advance of the actual need to store anything in them. Suppose you've decided that you absolutely want to work in the London office of your company by the end of next year.

Perhaps you haven't even announced your intentions to anyone. Nevertheless, place a file in your filing cabinet labeled "London."

Every time you see something about London, hereafter, instead of placing it in a random folder, you now have an easily accessible location. Maybe you have documents from the London office that you want to file, or there is something you want to hold on to related to travel planning. Later, perhaps you come across something related to housing that you'll want to keep as a reference.

You can create several file folders in advance based on the priorities you have identified and the goals you have established in support of those priorities. Here are some ideas for file folders of this kind:

- Retirement villages
- Vacation to Bali
- Day-care centers
- Palm-top computers
- Scholarships

Creating a file folder in advance of having anything to put into the folder is an affirmation of the goals you have chosen. At the least, it helps keep you organized. If you don't have such a folder, where are you going to put all of your papers? On top of a pile where it will be buried by whatever is placed on top? That's not a good idea.

What about your hard drive? The value of preemptive file folders is no less valid when it comes to organizing your hard drive. There may be a half dozen or so file folders that would be most appropriate for you to create based on where you are heading in your career and your life. When you create an empty file folder on your hard drive, especially when it's accessible off of another folder that you visit often, you get a frequent reminder that you do have a home for files as they emerge for this new topic area.

The tickler system works particularly well if you supervise a small staff of employees. Create a file folder for each person and name it for him or her. You can even create a file for yourself on your hard drive called "In Progress" that you open at the start of each day. The possibilities are endless! The point is for you to create space to house files so that you can quickly and easily retrieve what you need when you choose to.

Look upon establishing tickler files and files in advance of need as easy ways to become efficient in handling paper. Remain a lean and mean organizing machine. Keep your files thin but potent. Rather than seeing filing as drudgery, consider it a vital key to an organized career and life.

37

Pile It High

DESPITE ALL OF YOUR STERLING EFFORTS, you may be among those who find themselves continually confronted with visible signs of disorganization, such as piles and clutter. Take heart. The situation is not hopeless. First, gather all the tools you will need to enable you to break down those piles or disband that clutter. This could include file folders, rubber bands, paper clips, staplers, boxes, and so on. Piles and clutter don't magically go away, and they didn't magically accumulate (or did they?).

Allow yourself 30 minutes, or if that's too much, 15 minutes, to go through each item in the pile and assess what might best be done with it.

Recall the simple system for organizing things in tip #34. You have four options when confronting what to do with all of your stuff. You can:

- Act on it
- Delegate it
- File it
- Recycle or toss it

If you look through any given pile of stuff on your desk, chances are most of it can be recycled. You don't need to be hanging on to it. A lesser portion can probably be filed, and a slightly lesser portion of that can probably be delegated. That leaves you, hopefully, with a thin stack of things to act upon. With such organizing activity, when you stop and assess a pile or accumulation, you stand a far better chance of whittling out the unnecessary, and dealing with the rest (which usually represents a manageable amount).

Don't spend too much time deciding which file to place each item in. Simply make a quick assessment and go to the next item. Once your four piles are complete, undoubtedly you will notice that the "recycle" pile is the largest. The "file" pile, we can only hope, will be much smaller. The pile of stuff to delegate to other people is smaller still, and the file of things you need to act on is characteristically the smallest of all.

If you have six items competing for your time and attention, the most effective and efficient approach is to mercilessly mow them down one-by-one. You can rank them according to their importance, and work on number one to completion, or as far as you can take it, then proceed to number two, and so on. What's more, no other approach to handling six important and urgent items competing for your attention works as well as the method described above.

Proceed through the items that you need to act on and rank them according to what is most important. If an item is both urgent and important, put it at the top of the pile. If it is important, but not urgent, place it next. If it is simply urgent, place it after that. Finally, if it is neither urgent nor important, recycle, file, or delegate it. You'd be amazed at how many items belong in this category, such as specialized course offerings, new product announcements, or an article on management theory.

If you want to get into high gear, start tackling the items on the top of this final pile, which has the items you have deemed as being important and urgent. If you put the single most important and urgent item on top, the second in second place, the third in third place, and so forth, you are ready for high productivity.

Tackling the Important Pile—Once you're ready to begin working on the items in your important pile, list them all and make an estimate of how long it will take to complete each item. Then, add all the estimates together and multiply that number by 1.5. This compensates for your underestimation. Let's face it, things often take longer than we originally conceive. We don't know how long a project will take until we actually engage in it, at which time other issues sometimes arise!

If the number of task hours you face to complete the important pile grows to an astronomical figure, don't blow a mental fuse. It's not that the challenge has necessarily changed; you simply have better information regarding it. Marshal your resources accordingly. Realistically, what will it take to accomplish all that you have laid out before you as important and urgent, important, and so on? You may need additional staff help, or a bigger budget. In the short run, you may need to work longer hours.

As you approach the most important and urgent item, sometimes you simply can't take a task all the way to completion. Maybe it requires help from others. Maybe you need someone else to approve certain steps. Take it as far as you can go, and then consult with others. During the interim, however, start on the next project. Similarly, take that as far as you can go, to completion if you can.

Now and then, no matter how methodical your approach or well organized your desk or office, new items will compete for your time and attention, and conspire to upset your perfectly arranged kingdom. Such occurrences are expected—on a daily, if not hourly, basis.

As time passes, you'll find that you need a break from working on the important tasks that you have so carefully arranged. Again, this happens to everyone. You can only give your rapt attention and earnest efforts to the primo projects for so long, and then your mind starts to wander. You need a mental break. At this point, turn to items of lesser significance that don't require much mental effort. When you feel ready, return to the most important items, which are still situated conveniently on the top of the pile.

Continually strive to keep your piles as slim and trim as possible. You want to reduce the weight and volume of each pile by retaining only the highly relevant information and nothing more. For example, rather than retaining a 10-page report, hang on to only the single page that you actually need.

Taking this practice further, if you only need one paragraph, phone number, address, or Web site, then clip that specific portion and recycle the rest of the page. Attach the small clipping that you have retained to a sheet that contains other small relevant tidbits. Then, lay the assemblage down on the copier machine. You now have a dossier page that fully supports what you are working on, but doesn't take up much physical or psychological space.

Sometimes it does pay to let piles or accumulations mount up. When you receive a plethora of similar items, it's okay to let the pile grow for a while. Perhaps a stack of everything related to the competitor's product is accumulating on the corner table in your office. The pile is temporary and you intend to handle it completely, soon.

When that sacred time arrives, delve into the pile like a buzz saw. Discard duplicate information immediately. Combine like items, and then see which can be recycled as well. Pare down so that you have the slimmest, most potent file possible. When the pile is reasonably thin, peruse it again. Is there anything else that can be thrown out?

Pare Down and Win

YOU CAN PLAN YOUR DAY WITH THE SKILL AND PRECISION of a surgeon. Despite all the techniques discussed so far, mail, e-mail, Web sites, or phone calls will intrude at some point in the day. You will be accosted by material to be read, learned, or otherwise acted upon, thus throwing you off schedule. Each new intrusion can consume a few minutes or several hours. Added to everything else you're balancing, even small amounts of additional information can bring on feelings of frustration and anxiety.

How can you pare down a little at a time without breaking your stride? When you've finished a big project at work and you're not in the mindset to tackle some other major, intellectual pursuit at the moment, pare down your holdings as a form of transition. For example, if you recently finished a big report,

- Can you update any logs and reporting forms?
- Are there any memos or documents to send as a result of the finished report?
- Can you get rid of rough drafts and notes that are no longer applicable (notes you'll never use again)?

Be on the lookout for ways to continuously pare down your accumulations. "Kaizen," meaning continuous improvement, is an essential part of a Japanese philosophy about how to approach work. The seasoned kaizen practitioner seeks ways to make improvements that offer the most immediate and dramatic paybacks. Veterans know that such results cause you to look for even more ways to improve. The art of seeking continuous improvement is challenging, and in many cases, fun.

If your plans turn awry because it's pouring and the bridge is out, or the plane has been delayed for an hour and 10 minutes, in what small ways can you engage in continuous improvement? You can always pare down! Despite the availability of all manner of electronic gadgetry at your seat, I know high-powered executives who will have none of it. "None of it, I say!" Their airplane seat, they tell me, is among the few sanctuaries they have. It's where they get to open their briefcases and plow through them from A to Z, merging and purging, updating lists, getting rid of what is no longer necessary, and getting that little office in the air back into condition.

The same holds true if you commute by rail or bus. Use the little moments of the day to pare down. Instead of lugging around heavy issues of *Forbes*, *BusinessWeek*, or *The Wall Street Journal*, extract only the articles that appear relevant to you.

Merely reducing the volume of paper confronting you invariably is not the comprehensive answer to your organizational challenge. However, having addressed this issue as an author, professional speaker, and management consultant for 20 years, I'm thoroughly convinced that a reduction in the volume of paper is a tremendous boon to any quest to becoming organized. A slimmer file is easier to handle. Fewer notes in front of you mean fewer notes to contemplate. Fewer, but highly relevant research materials means less time reading, digesting, and applying what you have assembled. Any way you cut it, when you pare down, you increase the probability of succeeding in your organization quest.

Continue to Prune Your Files

The time and effort that you spend whittling what you no longer need pays off in many ways. For one, you physically have the space both within your desk and file cabinets and on your hard drive to accommodate new information, which, as we know by now, is well on its way. Chucking what you don't need gives you the opportunity to review that which you have filed and choose to retain:

• Contacts logged into your database may have left the area, perhaps passed away, or you know that you will never call on them again. Delete them without remorse from your database.

• Likewise, you can readily toss every piece of paper in your files relating to issues that are neither important, urgent, nor interesting. Keep the others in the aforementioned holding bin, or place where you park stuff that doesn't need to be seen or dealt with for the time being.

• On your hard drive, eliminate items that were once able to capture your attention, but now, after months or perhaps years, have overstayed their welcome.

• Examine your office. Are there gifts and mementos that you have received that hold little meaning for you or take up more space than they are worth? Are there books, reports, documents, and other items for which you still do not know the value? The chart below offers a quick look at what to retain versus what to toss:

Item	Feel Free to Toss or Recycle if . . .	Feel Free to Retain if . . .
Business cards, notes	You have many cards and never call anyone, or you can't recall the person, or the goods or services provided.	You already have a cardholder, can scan it, know you'll use it, or feel you will.
Papers, files, and documents	It's old, outdated, or uninformative, it's been transferred to disk.	It's your duty to retain it, you refer to it often, it has future value, or it comforts you.
Reports, magazines	It's old, outdated, stacking up, you think you need it to keep up, or you fear a quiz on it.	It's vital to your career or well-being, you choose to retain it, or there will be quiz on it.
Books, guides, directories	You've copied, scanned, or made notes on the key pages, it's obsolete, or has an updated version.	It's part of a life collection, you refer to it monthly, it has sentimental value, or you want it.

continued

Item	Feel Free to Toss or Recycle if . . .	Feel Free to Retain if . . .
CDs, DVDs, videos, cassettes	You never play it, and if you do, it doesn't evoke any feelings or memories. It plays poorly.	You play it, you like it, you couldn't bear to part with it. It's a keepsake.
Outdated office equipment	You know who would like it as a donation, you can sell it, it's collecting dust, or it's in the way.	It serves a specific purpose, it adds to the décor, or it can be overhauled or revitalized.
Mementos, memorabilia	It no longer holds meaning, you have many similar items, you do not have room, and you've changed.	It still evokes strong memories, you will hand it down someday, or it looks good on display.
Gifts, cards, presents	It's never in use, not wanted, and the bestowed won't know or be concerned that you tossed it.	You use it often, are glad you have it, or are saving it for some special reason.

Reduce Junk Mail

BOOKS ON TIME MANAGEMENT TRADITIONALLY DISCUSS how often to handle a piece of paper. I say that it always depends on what the paper says. When you make a purchase by mail, your name is sold and circulated to dozens of catalog houses. Notwithstanding, some companies repeatedly send huge amounts of junk mail, which wastes your time and clutters your life. So, how about some ideas to get these companies to stop tormenting you?

While you're trying to stay off of mailing lists and handle mail quickly, now and then you will be subject to mail from a repeat or gross offender. A gross offender is an organization that believes it has a God-given duty to continually inundate you with catalogs, brochures, and junk mail. Such parties merit special attention. If your name gets into the mailing list system, they're not likely to set you free. Hence, you need to apply strong medicine to those who would impede your desire to pare down, uncomplicate your life, and stay in control:

• When you're besieged by third-class mail from repeat or gross offenders, and such offenders have included a self-addressed bulk mail reply envelope, use the envelope to request that your name be removed from their lists. Also, review their literature or Web site to see if there is an 800 number you can use to make such a request at no cost.

• For those who don't heed your request, file a complaint with the Direct Marketing Association (DMA), the U.S. Postal Service, and the Office of the General Counsel of the offending group. After all, in an era when each piece of mail adds to environmental glut, it's your civic duty, as well as an effective technique for achieving breathing space, to reduce the amount of junk mail you receive. The DMA claims you can eliminate about 40 percent of your junk mail with one letter. Write to:

> *Mail Preference Service*
> *Direct Marketing Association*
> *P.O. Box 9008*
> *Farmingdale, NY   11735-9008*

Explain to them that you would "like my name removed from your direct mail lists." Sending this letter will effectively reduce your junk mail by 40 percent for three to six months. Thereafter, keep sending them the same letter. Here are some helpful tips to find out how to beat getting junk mail.

• To trace who is selling your name, when you make a mail order purchase or a donation, add a code to the end of your street address such as "1A" or "2D." Later, if you receive mail with your coded address, you know who sold your name to whom.

• When making any mail order purchase, feel free to mention or include a preprinted label that reads, "I don't want my name placed on any mailing lists whatsoever, and forbid the use, sale, rental, or transfer of my name."

• Sometimes the fastest way to deal with repeat offenders is to write the words "speed reply" right on the communication you've received. Underneath those two words write the message, "Please remove me from your mailing list now and forever." Sign your name, date it, and send back the same items or communication that you received. Be sure to address it to the mailing list manager of the offending organization.

• You can fight junk mail by saving all of it for weeks. Then hire a high school student at minimum wage to send a form letter to every party who has sent you mail more than once. Explain carefully that you have no interest in their offer.

• Some vendors ask for your name and address even when you pay in cash. Feel free to respectfully decline. If you want to be sly, give a false name and address.

• At all times and in all places, inform the parties with whom you do business that you do not appreciate having your name added to mailing lists, or being inundated by catalogs, announcements, brochures, and fliers. This is necessary if you place an order by fax, make a purchase by credit card, fill out a magazine subscription form, or procure any other type of good or service.

Read with Aplomb

UNDOUBTEDLY, READING HAS BECOME a major issue for you. The amount of reading you fathom to stay informed, further your career, or amuse yourself can be staggering. When you add it up, the piles can be daunting. In the course of a week you may find yourself spending anywhere from 10 to 20 hours simply on reading.

How can anyone today manage to stay organized in our overwhelming information society? Fortunately, there are many techniques that you can employ to assist you in completing your reading more swiftly, to help you organize what you need to retain, and still feel as if you have a life.

The quieter the place you find to read, the faster and easier you will be able to get through the pile. Yet, if you have some familiarity with what you are reading, even a somewhat noisy place can be an adequate environment. Find a quiet sanctuary whenever you are reading about highly technical issues, subjects with which you have little familiarity, heavy philosophical pieces, or anything about which you have to pause and reflect before proceeding. It's too difficult to do this kind of reading when you are surrounded by distractions.

You probably already know the value of reading early in the morning before others come into your office, or even earlier, before you leave your house. The same holds true for the evening, after everyone has left the office, or at home, after everyone else has retired. You can read faster and more thoroughly at these times.

Employ these techniques to improve your comprehension and speed:

• **Skimming.** Looking at the first couple of sentences of each paragraph within an article or chapter in a book is called skimming. By skimming you get to quickly find out whether you should read the article or chapter in greater depth. Simply skimming the first sentence or two is often all you need to gain the essence of the information being provided.

• **Scanning.** If you encounter a large volume of reading, such as a sizable book or a large report, it's not often practical to attempt skimming. With scanning, you quickly learn enough about the document to determine if it merits even greater attention. Scanning involves reviewing any list, chart, or exhibit in the book, the index, the table of contents, some of the chapter titles, foreword, and summaries.

Often, you can identify the handful of relevant passages or pages that are worth photocopying through scanning, and then recycle the remainder of the book or report. If you are concerned about the legality of photocopying, rest assured that if you are copying for a limited personal use then you are not violating any copyright laws.

•   **Evaluating the source.** The best sources routinely provide the best information. Rather than plow through dozens of industry journals, pick the best two or three, extracting articles of importance. You'll cut down on the total volume of what you need to read, while ensuring that you're being exposed to the best and latest of what's going on in your industry or profession.

•   **Assemble your tools.** If you use sticky pads, paper clips, felt tip pens, magic markers, scissors, and the like to assist you in your efforts when you read, then have them nearby. When you can deftly extract or highlight information you wish to retain, the overall reading burden is greatly reduced. Then you can maintain a lean, mean, potent file consisting of information and items that you will actually act upon or maybe retain.

•   **Cut books down to size.** Do you lament your lack of opportunity to tackle some of the current full-length books available? Unquestionably, there will be more full-length books than you want to read. Here is an organized method for approaching them in a highly productive manner:

1.   Read the back jacket in detail first. You'll see what others have said about the book. This may prompt you to make a more concerted effort once you turn to the pages within, or to abandon the book altogether—which could save you tons of time!

2.   Read the inside flaps of the book. The author usually writes this material. This is what the author wants you to know about the book and about him or herself.

3.   Read the foreword for more insight into what the book will teach, share, or explain to you.

4. Read the table of contents. Some chapters may be worth reading immediately. There may be other chapters you determine that you can safely skip.

5. Read the introduction, which is usually written by the author; it also provides the reader with a stronger sense of how the book came about, and why the author wrote it.

6. Proceed to the chapters you have decided are worth some attention and read the first two paragraphs to determine if you want to read the rest of the chapter. For those chapters where you don't want to continue, the first two paragraphs will at least give you a reasonable idea of what was covered.

7. Go to the last page of each chapter and read either the last paragraph or any summary or list of highlights presented. These can be invaluable and, in some cases, can serve as a substitute for reading the entire chapter.

8. Review any resource lists, reference lists, charts, or graphs that strike you as you are flipping through the book. Such features can be well worth the attention invested.

Finally, in the last chapter, read the last two pages. Often, the author's major conclusions and observations are presented here and this will save you reading at least the last chapter, possibly the last section of the book, or even the entire book. Always photocopy the handful of key pages that have value to you.

Whenever you encounter a review of a book, an excerpt, a critique, or anything else that gives you the essence of what the book says, you are ahead of the game. Many libraries stock books and lectures on tape, and in most cases, these represent abridged versions of the longer tome. You can safely listen to a cassette as you drive (an entirely different activity than talking on a cell phone). This is an easy way to gain information, avoid eyestrain, and still arrive on time.

When you suspect that a periodical subscription is worth the money, but not worth your time, let it go with the last issue. If you don't miss the publication, then you've got it made in the shade. If you do miss reading it, the publication will take you back, with open arms, often at a reduced rate. Perhaps you can gain the same information online, or visit the library periodically and peruse three or four issues of the same publication at high speed.

Part Five:

Organize Travel, Meetings, and Online Activities

Manage Your E-mail

YOU SEND AND RECEIVE E-MAILS ALL DAY LONG, and why not? E-mail is fast; it's transmitted nearly instantaneously after you push the send button. No paper, no toner cartridge, no stamps, no envelopes. No trip to the mailbox, no worrying about whether you had the right postage, no nothing. E-mail simply goes—which is why you receive so many every day. It's too convenient! You can send anything to anybody!

Mass delivery of spam has risen dramatically, despite software filters and Internet Service Provider (ISP) crackdowns on offenders. Using unsecured, third party servers, a spammer can target nearly every e-mail address found on the net at practically no cost, since ISP pays for the transmission. Some spammer sends a message of filth and smut with reckless abandon, knowing that if only a tiny fraction of targets respond, the venture can be profitable.

If you're receiving spam constantly along with regular e-mails, spending a brief time away from your PC allows a multitude of e-mails to pile up in your inbox, and that means you'll have scads of messages to respond to upon returning. Take a break for a mere two days, and you'll come back to at least two to three times the normal number of e-mail messages due to what I call the "law of e-mail accumulation," which states that the number of e-mails received increases exponentially with the number of days you are away from your computer.

I advocate practicing triage for all e-mail messages all the time. Triage is the method of quickly poring over a variety of items and allocating them based on what needs to be handled immediately, what can be handled later, and what can be ignored altogether. First, you want to eliminate the inane; this includes all forms of spam.

After you eliminate the obvious junk, pick out which e-mails you can place in a holding folder, bin, or file. Some messages are entirely worth saving but simply are not urgent. Some are from friends and loved ones, and you may want to read over their contents at leisure. Some will specify that a reply need not be immediate.

The final category is comprised of those e-mail messages you receive that require immediate action. The number of messages that fall under this heading should be small. These e-mails are not necessarily urgent; they may merely prompt action. If you're able to respond to a request quickly and effortlessly, why waste time parking it? If the message is staring you in the face, all you have to do is hit the reply button, type a few words, and then send it.

For those e-mails that mandate your present, earnest, and rather speedy attention, do your best to handle them so that you can be mentally free of them.

Organize Online Research

THERE ARE MORE THAN 3 BILLION WEB PAGES according to the directors at Google.com. Today, new, more user-friendly applications are becoming available all the time. The Internet is taking over as the dominant form of entertainment, communication, and information resource in society. Concurrently, it can become a major time drain.

On the heels of each problem related to Internet use comes application software and service-oriented sites that provide an antidote. Any specific program cited today will be quickly replaced, so instead, let's focus on broad categories:

•   **Bots:** You can download one of these little buggers from Web sites such as *www.botspots.com* and it will search the Internet all day long, giving you the best possible prices and best deals for the products and services you're seeking. The most popular bot is used for shopping, but they can also be used to ferret information on health, travel, and other bots!

•   **Mega search engines:** These enable you to type a keyword or key phrase and automatically engage in an intelligent search of the top search engines. For example, *Google.com* provides rosters of Web sites related to your search ranked by the number of links to each site instead of giving you listings according to the words that a site owner uses to describe his or her own site.

•   **Electronic clipping services:** "Clipping" services, including *www.luceonline.com* and *www.cyberclipping.com* offer you highly customized topic searches for a fee. For any single day, such sites can generate nearly everything that appears on the entire web about a given company or topic.

One good evening spent employing a handful of the most popular search engines could be what you need to create a dossier packet for yourself of high quality information and resources that could greatly accelerate your progress. If you don't have a PC at home, or if you aren't connected to the Internet, don't despair. Most libraries today provide Internet access to the public. If you have never connected to the Internet, the reference librarian can get you started in a matter of minutes.

Even if you are not familiar with a search engine, becoming proficient in working with one will usually require less than five minutes of your time. A PC connected to the Internet is the door to a world of new ideas. There are a variety of high quality sources at your fingertips that can assist you in making the changes necessary to get organized.

You must, however, protect yourself, and institute backup systems. A personal computer, for many people, is an expensive item. What happens when the computer malfunctions? Are you equipped to work without one? Do you have the money to replace a computer in the event of an accident?

Total backups include all files and all directories on a given drive. Selective backups are simply that, selective, and include only named or highlighted files and directories. Modified backups include only those files that have changed in any way since the last backup was done.

Computers don't require a lot of upkeep if you take a few simple precautions. For example, working in a clean, food-free environment is a good way to avoid an expensive repair bill for something that could have been prevented, and to eliminate the build up of crumbs in your keyboard. Treat your disks gingerly. Avoid leaving computer disks in direct sunlight or near heat. Disks are fragile, and if you accidentally leave one in your car, a hot summer's day can destroy all the information on it. Avoid magnets, which have a nagging tendency to suck the files off a disk into the abyss. Additionally, you may wish to put security measures and passwords in place so that unauthorized individuals do not have access to your information.

Still, you never know when a natural or manmade disaster is going to destroy your computer or the information in it. To avoid losing the wealth of information on your hard drive, create backup systems of your information frequently. Initiate a well-developed backup routine to save and store your valuable files. If you're not sure how to make a backup of your computer system, contact the company that produced your software or the manufacturer of your computer.

Keep backup disks or tapes in a fireproof cabinet, or some other secure place for safekeeping. Also, further protect your PC investment by purchasing a good power surge protector. Not all surge protectors are made the same way, so ask around before you buy, and always compare prices. The more valuable the information stored on your hard drive, and the more vital Internet access is to you for information-gathering and communication, the more important it is to safeguard this valuable resource.

Create More Organized Meetings, Really!

NOW, ON TO FACE-TO-FACE COMMUNICATIONS. Do you regard meetings as a massively unproductive way to pass the time? Or is that an understatement? Some people have such great dislike for meetings that they feel stressed and anxious the moment they learn they have to attend one, let alone conduct one. Despite the fact that many managers dislike calling meetings, and staff often dread attending them, studies show that people today are spending more time in meetings on a variety of topics with a variety of objectives than ever before.

Former Secretary of State Dr. Henry Kissinger felt that there was no purpose in having a meeting unless the desired outcomes were known in advance. The typical meeting is arranged by one person to convey information to many people. Ideally, the attendees will reflect upon what they heard, generate wonderful ideas, and take bold, decisive action to the delight of the meeting chair.

People shuffle into the meeting room and listen dully to some new stuff that they have to do, or learn, or take back to others. They also doodle, guzzle coffee, and manage to fall asleep. Most of what they hear is quickly forgotten. Whatever they're supposed to do is rarely done on time or in the fashion that the meeting manager had hoped for. There's got to be a better way—and there is.

A far more effective and organized way to conduct a meeting is to elicit the participation of those who will be a part of the meeting, long before it even starts. Yes, you read it correctly. It would only take two to four minutes per attendee for you to:

- Speak with people who will be attending the meeting
- Prep them for what will be discussed during the meeting
- Hear their views about what they're going to get out of the meeting
- Treat them as partners, not subjects

If your group meets on an ongoing basis, ask participants questions beforehand, such as:

- What methods have worked well for you in any previous meetings?
- How can we proceed in a manner that involves everyone?
- What would you like to get out of this meeting?

The above may sound like extra work. Consider, however, that meetings aren't held for the purpose of simply gathering a bunch of people into one place; they're held presumably to accomplish some worthwhile objective. If discussing meeting objectives with participants will greatly accelerate progress, why wouldn't you want to do this? The meeting is likely to take less time, which will result in greater participation and, ideally, greater advancement toward the desired objective. Moreover, participants actually report high enthusiasm for this process. It makes them feel important; they see that their input matters. They may anticipate the meeting with a new perspective, since they know that "this one" is going to be different.

Some managers dread the thought of having to preinterview meeting participants. "Gosh, talk to each person one at a time, how overwhelming." Yet, the process doesn't have to be strenuous if it's carried out in an organized fashion. Preinterviewing attendees gives you a leg up on exactly how to proceed:

1. You design a custom agenda that focuses on topics identified as important to the entire group.
2. You arrange the topics in an order conducive to achieving the group's overall objectives.
3. You circulate the agenda in advance so that participants come armed with ideas on how and when they can best contribute.

As a result, the meeting is far more likely to stay on course, end on time, and encourage participants to be more enthusiastic for the next meeting! And they regard you as an organized, competent manager. As you'll see with the very next meeting, when participants have a vested interest in the content of a meeting, they tend to arrive on time. When they receive an agenda in advance that specifies the precise starting time, they have yet another indicator of the importance of being there.

As a meeting manager, it behooves you to steadfastly start meetings on time so that stragglers will realize that they are late and that the others arrived as scheduled. Organized managers start meetings on time!

In his book *Breakthrough Business Meetings*, Robert Levasseur suggests that at the start of any meeting, "participants reach a common understanding of what they're going to do and how they're going to do it." Hence, everyone needs to be present at the start. Levasseur says that this normally consumes 10 percent of the meeting time, so if you're going to be in a meeting for 30 minutes, you only need three minutes or so to deal with some basic issues, such as:

- The main purpose of the meeting
- The participants' desired outcomes
- The actual agenda itself
- The key meeting roles, which for smaller groups is understood at the outset

After you make it clear that a strict start time is the norm, some individuals may still arrive tardy to meetings. There are several techniques, which work to varying degrees of effectiveness, to encourage promptness:

- In some organizations, tardy people have to apologize to the group. Then it becomes their responsibility afterward to catch up with the group for the parts they missed. Never backtrack for late arrivals; it will only subject everyone to stop and wait while the guilty party receives a personalized briefing.
- In some organizations, the meeting room doors are locked (only for the bold!). Anyone who tries to enter late has to knock on the door. Depending on how charitable you're feeling, the knocks may or may not be answered on the first round. Tardy attendees then sheepishly take their seats.
- In some organizations, plum assignments are handed out in the first few minutes so that tardy people are left with the least desirable tasks. This is a great incentive for arriving early. In certain organizations, and this is not my preference, the tardy are the subject of early discussion. In other words, they are the target of gossip, innuendoes, and jokes.

In my first job, if you were late for a meeting, you had to throw a dollar into the kitty for every minute you were late. Sure as heck, nobody ever walked in more than five minutes late. (I have no idea what they used the money for!)

You may quickly catch on that none of these subtle coercions are as effective as preinterviewing participants, circulating an agenda, and demonstrating on a repeated basis that the meetings start promptly as scheduled.

Maintain Effective Meetings, the Whole Way!

WHEN PARTICIPANTS KNOW IN ADVANCE that a particular item will be allotted five minutes, most people do their best to honor that time frame. Hence, a strong, organized agenda in the best possible sequence, and with estimated time frames for each agenda item is the winning formula for keeping meetings on track.

You follow the agenda, eliciting the input of others as needed. You encourage attendees to participate. As each agenda item is discussed, ask participants to keep in mind the following questions: What is the specific issue being discussed? What does the group want to accomplish in discussing the item? What action needs to be taken to handle the issue?

When the necessary action is identified, key questions include: Who will act? What resources do he or she require? When will the issue be resolved? When will the group discuss the results? Upon successful conclusion of these questions, the group then moves on to the next issue.

Not all issues require proceeding through every question. Sometimes an agenda item merely represents an announcement or a report to the group that doesn't require any feedback or discussion. Sometimes the issue at hand represents an executive briefing, because the matter has already been resolved. On occasion, unnecessary discussion ensues, and an item ends up requiring twice as much time as originally allotted. Often, however, participants make up for the overflow in one area by being briefer in other areas.

When you are addressing a group whose participants have been preinterviewed and an agenda has been circulated in advance, there are a variety of techniques you can use to keep the meeting organized and on track. Each technique will vary in effectiveness, depending on the purpose of your group, how often it meets, and your group's history. Consider some of the following suggestions for your meetings:

• Require participants to keep their remarks within an allotted time frame. Some groups keep a timer in plain view of all participants to encourage them to keep their comments brief. Others meet in a room with a wall clock in view.

• Have the meeting manager announce who will be speaking next and how many minutes have been allocated for the topic on the agenda.

• Ask participants to circulate summaries of their comments, charts, or exhibits in advance that illustrate the points they wish to make. Then, have them offer brief commentary to highlight the information in distributed materials.

When you preassign times to each issue, participants may actually seek to stay within those time frames! When you elicit time frames from the participants in advance, then it behooves them to stay on track. If someone admits in advance that only three minutes are needed for a particular issue, then that individual is less likely to run on and on and on . . . Here are other ideas to keep meetings organized and on course:

•   Encourage meeting participants to arrive early and stay late. Then they are more likely to get down to business during the meeting because they have time to banter and joke around both before and after the meeting (as opposed to during the meeting).

•   Ask participants to stand when they speak. This tends to limit the time that they speak, because most people prefer to stay seated. Also, much time will be saved if people merely stand at their chairs and speak instead of ambling to the front of the room.

•   Request that those who can't be in attendance submit what they would have said in a concise paragraph or two to be read by someone in attendance.

The organized meeting manager knows the importance of building some slack into all meetings. For example, a manager may allocate five minutes for a topic that he or she will personally be covering, knowing that it will actually require about three minutes. Hence, several minutes can be saved here and there. So, even if somebody goes over the allotted time frame, the meeting still stays on track and ends on time. What a world.

Meet to Achieve Results

SOME GROUPS MEET WITH AN ACCOUNTANT, an attorney, or another advisor as a method of keeping the meeting on track and headed toward the desired objectives. International Toastmaster meetings, for example, include a parliamentarian who routinely advises the group as to when they have strayed from established protocol. Some groups choose to have one person serve as timer. Also, you or some other designated attendee may decide when a matter is best handled by a smaller group, like a task force or selected team.

For those items on the agenda that have a corresponding objective, you have the responsibility to track the progress. What else needs to be accomplished, and by when, to meet the overall objective? As with any goal or objective (see tip #19), they need to be:

- Written down
- Quantified
- Assigned specific time frames

The quickest way to lose the participants, other than being an interminable, crashing bore, is to conduct your meeting in a room where the temperature is too high, or where ventilation is poor. That, coupled with a dark meeting room, encourages people to fall asleep. It's an anthropological phenomenon—as soon as it's dark, the brain gets the message that it's okay to doze off. A warm, stuffy room only aids the process.

You always want to meet in a well-lit room with excellent venti-lation. If you have a choice between having a room slightly too warm or slightly too cool, opt for cool. A cool room will keep par-ticipants fresh and alert. The discomfort may prompt attendees to complain and a little frostbite might result, but at least no one will go to sleep. If participants need to take written notes or work from laptop computers, make sure there are effective flat surfaces on which they can work. Pens, pads, cold water, and possibly tea or coffee should also be available. In some groups, the secretary or transcriber takes notes on everything that is being said. Other groups use the far more efficient tape recorder and have the notes transcribed afterward.

Whatever your recording method is, set up and check out tape recorders, pocket dictators, overhead projectors, slides, chalkboards, whiteboards, and all other equipment far before the meeting begins. Also check for replacement batteries, light bulbs, extension cords, and all supporting equipment in advance.

If your meeting lasts longer than 30 minutes, schedule breaks some time in the middle, so as not to lose the attention of your par-ticipants. You may also lose their attention simply because attention spans in this day and age are only so long.

Here are some other room organizing techniques for conducting a meeting:

• Meet in a room where participants won't be disturbed by ringing phones, people knocking on the door, and other intrusions. You want to achieve a meeting of the minds and accomplish great things; distractions do not help.

• Meet where there is wall-to-wall carpeting and walls adorned with pictures, posters, and the like to help absorb sounds and offer a richer texture to the voices being heard. Contrast this environment with a meeting held in a room with a tile floor, cold metal chairs, and blank, thin walls. Participants can't wait for the meeting to be over when the meeting room feels like a holding cell, no matter what's being discussed.

- Meet where the seats are comfortable and supportive. However, overly comfortable seats may have a detrimental effect and encourage people to nod off. Ideally, everyone's seat would be the same, with none higher or lower than any other.

Maintain a supportive atmosphere for all participants; otherwise, comments come off as edicts (i.e., "I say, you do"). Edicts don't encourage people to attend meetings in the future, even when something vital and interesting is being presented.

Serve as a facilitator. You elicit the best of responses from participants, encouraging them to cooperate with one another, and encouraging them to truly function as a team. In the smallest of groups, as well as in larger gatherings, the diverse backgrounds and personalities of participants ensure that there will be clashes on occasion. Help keep the disruption to a minimum.

Too many managers, in the erroneous attempt to "save time," don't bother to gather any feedback from participants following a meeting. They figure that their own observations were plenty, so why bother taking the time to consult with others? Organized and effective meeting managers have the courage to engage in meeting follow-up. They speak with participants afterward to learn if participants thought the meeting was effective, what could be added, what could be dropped, and how it could be improved.

The manager then takes these suggestions back, ruminates on them, and actually incorporates into the next meeting, those that would make a significant contribution. If meeting participants are assigned to reach an objective, they realize the meeting manager can facilitate that by having more effective meetings. Ultimately, listening to feedback from participants is a time saver for the manager.

Organize for the Road

IN EVERY METROPOLITAN AND SUBURBAN AREA throughout the United States, and increasingly in traffic throughout the world, commuting has become drudgery. You crawl along bumper to bumper, inhaling the fumes of the thousands of cars on a superhighway that effectively operates like a slow moving parking lot.

When you're driving a car, even at a crawl, your principal activity is driving. A study published by the *New England Journal of Medicine* showed that driving while speaking on a cell phone makes you four times as likely to get into an accident and 11 times as likely to be killed while driving. You can only focus your sharp attention in one basic direction.

If you're at a traffic light or sitting in slowly moving traffic, it is still dangerous to talk on a cell phone, even a hands-free cell phone with a speaker. Pull off to the side of the road if you can't function without making a call. (Gee, how did drivers manage for the first 100 years?!)

Conversely, listening to the radio or a CD, or speaking with someone in the passenger seat does not pose the same risk. Your sharp attention can continue to be on the road even as you tune in to the radio, a CD, or the passenger in the seat next to you. This is because, at any given moment, your driving takes precedence. This is not the case with the use of the cell phone—concentrating on the conversation with someone at a distance and driving compete with one another.

If you are going to ride with others on the way to work as part of a carpool or vanpool, choose people you like to talk to. Surprisingly, you may have more lively conversations with someone who does not work with you, and you will both benefit from the conversation.

Close your windows for a quieter ride and better control of your environment. If you decide to listen to something, play an invigorating or inspiring CD or cassette tape. Investigate services such as books on tape. Visit your library and find lectures, plays, and essays on audio. Or turn on some classical music; the rhythms and composition have been shown to promote healing and well-being, unlike other forms of music, which can have a disconcerting effect.

Now, to the matter of organizing your vehicle—keeping your car in top running condition is the major prerequisite to success on the road. You only have to break down once in a strange location to experience how unproductive a day can be. Take your car in for a tune-up on a regular basis, as the manufacturer recommends. Bring it in any time you even suspect that something is not operating as it ought to be.

Whether the traffic is moving quickly or slowly, use commuting time to contemplate your day. A major key to personal effectiveness while commuting is to use that time for reflection. Instead of automatically flipping on the radio, you can organize your thoughts en route to your various destinations. Consider what's on your agenda for the morning, what you'll be doing, whom you will be meeting, and then see yourself successfully handling it all. Contemplate eating your lunch, coming back from lunch, having appointments, taking care of projects, meeting with others, or other imminent activities.

Navigate Errands While Commuting

Here is a masterstroke of organizing effectiveness: Instead of letting all your errands stack up for the weekends, designate one night per week as "errand night." Make, for example, a Monday, Tuesday, or Wednesday the night on which you will handle errands on the way back from work.

Prepare for multiple stops. You may wish to make a brief list of your errands and affix it to your dashboard. Keep a file folder, envelope, or pouch handy for assembling the various tickets, sales slips, and so forth that you will be dispensing and collecting. If you can, keep the passenger side of your car clear so that it serves as your command center on wheels.

If you encounter traffic backups and long lines or other undue delays while making your errand run, fold up the tent and head home. It's no use trying to force your way through the crowds. You can get your stress in other ways. You can always handle errands another night, still preserve your weekends, and get everything done in less time and with less hassle.

Buy in multiples so you don't have to return to various stores as often. When it is practical, go on the Internet, and find vendors who pick up and deliver (see tip #42). Have vendors come to you.

Rather than picking up stamps at the post office, order them by mail. Rather than dropping off deposits at the bank, mail them in. Every time that you don't have to get into your car to accomplish something, you save time, preserve your vehicle, and preserve your sanity. As more of what you need to do is accessible via catalogs and the Internet, you may find that only a couple of hours a week is more than enough time to take care of the errands for which you need to be physically present.

47

Handle Commuting and Travel Contingencies

DO YOU CLAW YOUR WAY INTO WORK, MILE BY MILE? To avoid the masses in the morning and afternoon, depart when everyone else isn't. If you can head out on the road an hour or an hour-and-a-half earlier than everyone else, or for that matter, an hour or an hour-and-a-half later, you're likely to have smoother sailing.

Consider getting up at your normal time, working for an hour-and-a-half at home, and then departing for the office. Maybe you can leave work early in the afternoon, arrive home without fighting a lot of traffic, and then continue with your work at home. Perhaps you prefer to leave after everyone else does at the end of the day. To keep yourself on track, put a few key items in your car in advance.

Attach an extra set of car keys someplace under the bumper in one of those magnetic hide-a-key compartments. Also, have spare house keys hidden in your car, as you would have spare car keys somewhere in your house. Getting locked out is not productive. Calling somebody to open your car is a waste of time and money. Hide a roll of dimes and quarters in your car since parking meters, pay phones, and vending machines gobble them up.

Put a backup briefcase or folder in your trunk with stamps, envelopes, a pen, paper, a calculator, and perhaps important phone numbers. If you ride with a cell phone or notebook or palm-top computer, undoubtedly you have key addresses and key phone numbers with you. If not, hide important phone numbers, pin numbers, and access numbers someplace in your car where they will never be found by anyone else, but where you can draw upon them in a hurry if you need to.

What else is worth storing in the car? You may store a gym bag with socks, extra underwear, a toothbrush, tissues, flashlight, sunglasses, credit cards, maps of the area, library cards, first aid kit, umbrella, a raincoat, a hat, and some gloves, among other things. I also keep an extra, concealed wallet with credit cards and a container of gas additive in my car. It's also a good idea to keep a blanket in your car in case you are stranded someplace where it is cold. When you become acutely aware of the cost of being locked out of your car, delayed, or stuck in the city unprepared, you'll get prepared.

If you're not a member of one of the national auto clubs, consider the advantages of joining. If your car needs a jump-start or tow only once per year, the annual cost of membership will pay for itself. Having this kind of security is priceless. By dialing an 800 number, you can have a top-flight garage with a qualified towing specialist on the scene usually in 45 minutes or less almost wherever you are.

Once a week, if you can, telecommute—avoid going into the office at all. Get wired to your office by fax, modem, and telephone if you're not already. If you stay home even one Wednesday every other week, you're far more productive in handling the kinds of tasks that are hard to tackle in a hectic office. Plus, you can wear your pajamas all day.

48

Be Productive on Public Transportation

IF YOU ARE AMONG THE LESS THAN 10 PERCENT of the working population who get to work via public transportation, my hat's off to you. Though cities have designed vast subway and bus systems, the majority of commuters still get to work by automobile. There are many ways to be productive while on a bus, subway, train, or in a van. You already know most of them, so we will be brief here.

To tune out surrounding noise on a mass transit system, use a portable cassette or CD player. Choose what you want to listen to, but make sure that it's uplifting, informative, and generally supports how you want to be and feel in life. If you choose to read the newspaper, that's fine. If you're reading this book right now on the train, more power to you!

If you travel with a palm-top or notebook computer, you probably already have your routine down pat. Depending on the brightness of your screen, you may wish to sit on the nonsunny side of the vehicle. Supply yourself with plenty of recharged batteries for the ride.

Do not house your expensive computer in a traditional carrying case; these are ready-made targets for thieves. Instead, carry expensive equipment in a satchel, a rather worn briefcase, or some other ratty carrying case that looks like it would be used to house anything but a computer.

The lighter you travel, the more adept you will be at getting on and off the bus, subway, train, or other vehicle. If you have been commuting for any length of time, you know how long the ride will take, so you can plan your work accordingly. I've seen many adept professionals practice what I call vest pocket management. They are able to pull out a pad or pen, business cards, sticky notes, a palmtop computer, a handheld calendar, a pocket dictator, or a variety of other work-related tools from their vest pockets. They can get to work at the drop of a hat, and pack up as quickly.

If you read voraciously during your time on public transportation, stay lean and mean. When plowing through magazines, quickly tear out those articles that seem to be of interest, those that represent something important and urgent, or at least important, and recycle the rest of the magazine. Your goal while traveling is to always have less at the end of your trip to carry.

Retain the smallest volume of paper that serves your purposes. For example, if you only need a Web site address, a phone number, or a key bit of information, don't save pages and pages from an article. Instead, save the one key page that contains the information you need.

The availability of handheld scanners makes it possible to travel with a pocket scanner, scan in one line at a time, and end up carrying exceedingly little paper. In addition, if you travel with a pocket dictator, simply record the key phrases, phone numbers, and other tidbits of information you wish to retain. Later you can transcribe your own tape, or better yet, have someone else transcribe it, and transfer the information to hard disk.

If you travel with a cell phone or a pocket dictator, be respectful of other passengers. Turn away from the open area, modulate your voice, and keep your conversations as short as possible. You may be taking care of all kinds of business with your sleek little phone, but to everyone else in hearing range, you are a noisy offender.

Checking for voice mail messages, e-mail, and other correspondence can, of course, all be easily handled while in transit. But don't whip yourself into a frenzy over the gathering of these messages. They'll still be there when you arrive at your destination.

49

Fly Friendlier Skies

WITH THE INCREASE IN PASSENGERS, more restrictive airline configuration, and tightened security, airline travel has become a true pain. The key to staying organized and productive before, during, and after flying is to stay light and take care of as many things as you can in advance.

- Pack the night before and pack as light as you can
- Use the least number of toiletries
- Use rolling luggage to avoid having to lift your heavy bag

Most airlines will accept carryon luggage of 22 inches by 14 inches by 9 inches. Thus, you can roll your luggage onto the plane and never have to check your bag, saving a good 15 to 20 minutes prior to your departure, and upon arrival at your destination. If you have to pack a second bag, use something that fits on the top of your rolling cart luggage; essentially, you are not lifting either bag, but rolling them both.

Many airlines will accept two bags and still let you take them on board. If you have to have more than two bags, you might as well check them all, since waiting for one bag takes up about as much time as waiting for all your bags.

If you have a lengthy trip with many stops, rather than trying to bring clothes for each day, bring enough clothing for half the trip plus one day. In other words, if you are traveling for nine days, bring five days worth of clothing. If you are traveling for ten days, bring six days' worth of clothing. Then, as you approach the halfway point of your trip, get everything cleaned while on the road. Taking advantage of laundry and valet services costs a little money, but you're better off shelling out a few dollars here and there than toting around a bulky bag of heavy clothing.

Keep your briefcase packed lightly and efficiently. Bring Priority Mail packages with you so that as you collect documents and information during your travels you can mail them back to yourself rather than continuing to carry them. At fewer than $4, the Priority Mail package is relatively inexpensive. Bring address labels for both your destination and your home base. This saves you from writing your name and address over and over.

Don't pack anything that you know your hotel or host destination already supplies. You can always call in advance to get the list of what is offered. It can be a great boon if you don't have to pack a bathrobe, an alarm clock, a hairdryer, and other overnight necessities. Save the little soaps and other toiletries the hotel offers. The little weight and volume is ideal for subsequent trips, and they come in handy.

Book Your Flight Right

IF YOU ENJOY LONG LINES AND MAJOR GRIEF, buy tickets at the airline ticket counter the day of your departure. If you do, you are likely to get the worst seats at the highest price. Bad seating will negatively impact your productivity and use of time while on board. You want to buy your tickets in advance so that you can get a bulkhead, a wing row, or an aisle seat. Each of these offers more room than the middle seat or the window location.

Always bring a water bottle with you so that you do not have to wait for flight attendants to come around to quench your thirst. A few sips here and there can make all the difference between maintaining high energy and high productivity, and being sluggish, dehydrated, and not able to get quality work completed.

Bring your own snacks. Yes, pack your own food and don't scowl! What do you bring? You can bring carrots, cucumbers, apples, bananas, sunflower seeds, peanuts, and anything else that is healthy, and will give you an energy boost. Avoid bringing candy, cupcakes, and other heavily sugared or salted items, such as pretzels, prepackaged cheese and crackers, and other widely commercially available snack foods that offer nothing more than dead carbohydrates. These will drain you of energy, leave your body nutrient-starved, and cause you to operate with far less efficiency than is otherwise possible.

Sitting in an airplane seat for hours on end has always been confining. Avoid heavy clothing, tight shoes, restrictive belts, and anything else that reduces respiration, ventilation, and circulation. If you're meeting a client as soon as you land at your destination, you may have to sacrifice wearing what you want by wearing a suit or dressy attire. Otherwise, wear loose and comfortable clothing. You want to be able to move around freely and enjoy the flight.

If you are flying in the middle of the day when the sun's ultraviolet rays are more pronounced, make sure you have your sunglasses with you. Also use the airline overhead lighting and lower your window cover. Your eyes won't get nearly as fatigued. In our highly mobile society, the chances are increasing that you will be spending time in a moving vehicle. By making adequate preparations in advance, you maximize your potential for being at your best while in motion and afterward.

Part Six:

Making Your Home Your Castle

Destroy Enemy Outposts

THE ACTIVITIES REQUIRED TO KEEP A DEN OR CAR ORGANIZED are basically no different than the activities that you already engage in at the places that you have no difficulty keeping organized. Simply apply the best of what you are doing in one place or space to another and you'll find that staying organized is not such an arduous task.

Getting organized in your personal life supports your efforts in your professional life. The more organized you are at home, at work, and in other places in your life, the greater the probability that you will have more focus, energy, and direction when you head into work. You will certainly be more efficient, and perhaps have greater peace of mind.

To ensure that your home environment enhances your sense of control, don't allow ad hoc outposts to build up. Adopt supportive docking and unloading techniques. Always bring mail, office work you've brought home, tax receipts, and newly purchased items (including warranties and tags) to their final destinations or to your administrative outpost for processing and integration into your organization system.

The more often you're able to keep the surfaces, such as the dining room table, your desk, and small tables clear, the greater your ability to manage the flow of items in your life, deal with them capably, and move on.

Q: So, remaining organized starts when I come in the door?

A: Yes. Avoid leaving things at inappropriate outposts. Take items to their end destinations when you get home, or shortly thereafter. If an item belongs in the den, take it to the den. If it belongs in the closet, go to the closet.

When you fail to take items to their end destinations, you create double and triple the work for yourself. Do you want to do that to yourself? The piling up of little unfinished chores can make you feel overwhelmed. Upon returning from travel, immediately unpack your bags, put clothes in the closet or washer, and take all paperwork to your desk.

If you keep a small cabinet or table by the door, use it only for what is leaving your home, never for what is entering. What enters goes directly to its final resting place. What exits departs soon. The process is continual.

If mornings are a super rush for you, lighten your load by reducing the number of items you have to round up and things you have to do. Visit your car the night before and stock it as fully as possible with the items you or your crew need for the next day. This includes office files, books, gym clothes, and lunch bags—whatever doesn't spoil.

At home, if your closets are jam-packed with all sorts of stuff you have stowed over the years, it's time to engage in spring cleaning, whether spring is here or not. If you can't bear to part with all the stuff you've crammed in there, at least separate it by the seasons.

As spring approaches, box up all the winter items and put them in an out-of-the-way part of the house. Perhaps they can go into the attic, the basement, or some infrequently used room. It should take you 60 minutes or less for each closet. Once they are organized, they are set for at least a season.

As you proceed through your house reclaiming spaces, you'll find the payoff spills over into your career. The 21st century man or woman is simply inundated with too many items competing for time and attention, whether it is at work, at home, or in between. Cramming an unreasonable number of activities into a given unit of time perceptually tends to make that time speed by. Likewise, cramming too many items into a physical space tends to make you feel out of control.

By banishing enemy outposts and reclaiming your spaces, you can find things faster and easier, save time, depart more easily in the morning, and stow things more easily at the end of the day.

Pick a Regular Day and Time

WHEN IT COMES TO PUTTING ONE'S HOME IN ORDER, some people find the workweek to be too hectic, so they wait until Friday evening or Saturday morning. Rhonda, for example, is too exhausted during the week and on Friday evening to even entertain the idea of putting her house in order. After a good night's rest on Friday, however, she is revived and ready to go.

She starts the wash soon after rising and then vacuums the house as the washing machine is going through its cycles. When the wash cycle is finished, she puts the clothes in the dryer and then begins working in the kitchen, handling any dirty dishes and silverware, cleaning the sink, and sweeping the floor. By the time it becomes necessary to take the clothes out of the dryer and fold them, she is approaching the finish line of her Saturday morning ritual.

As Rhonda distributes items to the linen closet, bedroom drawers, and closets, she straightens up each of these rooms quickly. Then she finishes cleaning the two bathrooms in her home. In 90 minutes or thereabouts, presto! Her work is done. Thereafter, only a few maintenance activities are necessary during the rest of Saturday and Sunday, and with enough nagging, she can get her husband to do those. In any event, she does her best to hold the line during the week.

Invariably, by next Friday the house is a mess again. Not to worry. Rhonda does not stress out because she maintains a regular day and time when she puts things in order. If she's away one Saturday morning or some circumstance arises, she temporarily rearranges her schedule and maintains order nonetheless.

In your own situation at work or at home, pick a regular day and time, like Rhonda, and you too can maintain order. You might even be the first on your block.

Many career professionals devote some part of Friday afternoon to "office housekeeping" if they don't already have some pressing assignment or deadline. Actually, Friday afternoon is a stupendous time to refile and straighten up the desk and surrounding areas. Why Friday? For many people there is more noise in the office on that day than on any other. Also, some people have a hard time staying focused as the last few hours of the workweek approach.

If others in your office adopt the habit of straightening up on Fridays, then it's all the more convenient for you to do so as well. You'll be part of the office milieu. Then you can leave for the weekend with a sense of control over your professional environment.

Regardless of the day and the time you choose, develop an organizing maintenance routine. You'll find that those onerous, recurring, organizing-related tasks are not so big and, all told, not so bad.

53

Approach Spaces Strategically

THINK STRATEGICALLY WHEN APPROACHING YOUR SPACES. For example, consider your linen closet. The linen closet is a restricted space for storage of your linens and towels. Organize them in a way such that all you have to do is open the door and, behold, the items that you need are at your fingertips.

To easily maintain order, store all towels of the same size together. Avoid stowing frequently used items on high shelves. If towels and washcloths will be retrieved from the linen closet every day or every other day, it makes sense to have them be accessible to everyone who needs them, including shorter people and small children.

Your linen closet can contain a variety of other things besides linens, towels, and washcloths. This includes anything that is not easily stored within the bathroom. You don't want your linen closet overflowing with bathroom supplies; however, you can make it complement your bathroom, housing those items for which there is no additional room in the bathroom. For example:

• Stow some of the larger items that cannot be stored easily in the bathroom, such as a hair dryer or other electrical devices, in the linen closet.

• Employ small boxes to keep a variety of supplies neatly organized. These items could include extra soap, shampoo, toothpaste, and various personal hygiene items.

• Use the height of shelves to determine what goes where. For example, if you have small children and you want them to be able to reach washcloths, these would go on lower shelves. Alternatively, if there are items that children should not be touching, these would go on the highest shelves.

Some people use the far reaches of the linen closet to store extra supplies, while they stack their towels, washcloths, bed sheets, or pillowcases closer to the front of each shelf. When you open the linen closet, you should only see fabric items. It may seem like a small point, but sometimes visually arranging the closet is as helpful as anything else you can do to maintain the feeling of being in control. When you strategically approach your linen closet or any other of your vital spaces, you have a better chance of devising an orderly system that will serve you well.

Apply strategic thinking to other areas of your home. If you can't see the floor of your closet, organize your shoes. You can get creative on this one. You can buy ready-built shoe caddies at most discount stores or simply use a shoe bag. You can even use old wine racks to hold shoes. If you get a shoe bag you can hang it on the wall in your closet or on the back of the door. Shoe bags made of a mesh material are particularly useful because you can see which shoes are in which compartment, and you don't have to bend over to find them.

Visit a store such as Bed, Bath and Beyond, Hold Your Own, or any of the other home center stores dotting the horizon and you'll encounter a variety of "shoe organizing" systems. Take measurements of your closets in advance so that you can determine which of these devices might comfortably fit within the space that you have. One of the grandest shoe organizing techniques is giving away those that you don't wear anymore.

Undoubtedly, you have community groups that would gladly accept donations of shoes, including Goodwill, the Salvation Army, and if you belong to one, your own church. Be honest with yourself in deciding what shoes you will actually wear, and what shoes can safely be given away. Otherwise, the seldom worn shoes will populate your closet for the rest of your days. You will feel good about giving away the excess shoes, and if the spirit moves you, you will have more room available for acquiring new shoes!

54

Adopt a Replacement Policy

AS YOU BEGIN REGAINING SOME ORDER IN YOUR LIFE, here is an insightful and practical way to keep accumulations from engulfing you: Employ the replacement principle. When you acquire something new, something else has to go. The chart below offers examples of nonreplacement policies contrasted with replacement policies.

Nonreplacement Policies	Replacement Policies
Your child's collection of DVDs grows to beyond 50 as you buy or copy the classic and latest hits.	You decide with your child in advance on a total number of DVDs he or she can have. Each new one means replacing an old one.
Your file cabinet keeps growing until you need to buy another.	Your files stay the same size, because for each item you add, you discard one.
Old equipment can be found in closets and storage bins. You hang on to it thinking it's going to have future value.	When you buy new equipment, you donate older, less efficient equipment to a charitable organization and get a tax deduction.

continued

Nonreplacement Policies	**Replacement Policies**
You've collected books since college and now have overflowing shelves with no hope of reading most of what you've collected.	You retain only books of continuing or sentimental value. You quickly scan most books or copy the pages that are most important to you, and give them away.
Although you have an 84GB hard disk, you are considering getting more disk space.	You don't need any additional hard disk space, because at least monthly, you routinely prune your disk of out dated files.
You have a collection of annual reports, 401(k) statements, and the like from investment houses, most of which you haven't read.	When you receive an annual report from an investment firm, you quickly replace what they sent you last year with the new one.
Your clothes drawers and closets are overfilled, mostly with items you haven't worn in years.	There is more than sufficient space to house the clothes that you actually use, because you give the rest to charities.
You have a ton of brochures and memorabilia from your last trip, and many previous trips as well.	You have a few choice mementos from your last several trips, and you've chosen to display some of them and store the rest.
Your record collection spans many shelves and is covered with dust; you hardly ever play them.	You sell/trash/donate those LPs and buy a few "greatest hits" CDs you know you will play and enjoy.

If you're not constantly reducing what you're holding on to, you're not acknowledging the reality of an era that keeps throwing more at you than you can respond to.

55

Improvise When Storage Space Is Limited

FACE IT, YOU PROBABLY FIND that you'll never have all the space you need. Based on that, you'll need to improvise. Consider a home that lacks a full or even partial basement, but does have a tiny cellar that is only big enough to accommodate one person in it at a time. Organization techniques in this space will also serve you well.

- Ensure that the small cellar is easily accessible, whether from inside your home or from an exterior entrance.
- Install a light nearby on a switch. If this is not feasible, use a dependable flashlight or suitable substitute.
- Don't keep anything on the steps as it will almost inevitably cause someone to trip and fall.
- If floor space is limited, use the walls. Securely fasten supplies, tools, and other suitable items to the wall.
- Keep the area clean. Such cellars often accumulate dust and dirt in a hurry.

If you need more storage space, consider freestanding storage units, which are available in varying sizes from hardware and home center stores at a surprisingly affordable price. Storage units may come preassembled or in modular form that you can assemble on your own. Most often they are not heated. However, they enable you to maintain a fine level of organization because you can store things in them that otherwise clutter your garage or other storage areas attached to your home.

As with the small cellar, or garage for that matter, keep the storage area clean; use wall space to maximum advantage, and allow yourself the ability to easily maneuver within the storage unit. You don't want to be bumping into or falling over things.

Keep the center of the storage unit clear and arrange your possessions around the facility in a U-type configuration. This will provide you with access to everything and you won't have to reach over something to get to something else.

Don't fall into the trap of overloading, like too many people, with cellars or other storage facilities in and around their homes. It starts off harmless enough, and for the first few months or even years, everything seems orderly. Surely, before you know it, these spaces are jam-packed with stuff. Suddenly, it seems as if you have inadequate storage space!

Ah, but do you? You haven't cleaned out your storage room in the longest time. Such places represent hazards to those who dare to venture in. Some of these storage areas are firetraps containing flammable materials. Others represent accidents waiting to happen—there may be tools with sharp points that might injure unsuspecting visitors. Take control of these spaces now before anyone gets hurt. In such cases, a little organization goes a long, long way!

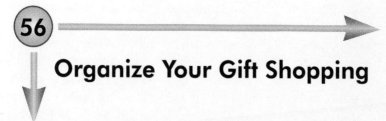

56

Organize Your Gift Shopping

IT'S DIFFICULT TO BUY PRESENTS FOR SOME PEOPLE (and you know who they are!). Instead of feeling flustered the next time the look on a recipient's face betrays his or her true feelings about the gift, you should rethink how you shop. Adjusting how and when you shop can make buying less stressful for you. Moreover, you'll be more likely to buy a gift that's appreciated.

One of the most difficult chores at holiday time is finding the right gift for friends and family. Some people are easy to buy for, but there are those who are picky and those you don't know that well. Create a year-round holiday gift list to ease the burden of shopping. When a friend comments on something he or she likes, make note of it.

Carefully pick the days you shop. Mondays and Tuesdays are much less crowded than the weekends. If you work away from home, you may have to shop in the evenings. Since you'll be tired after your hectic workday, buy smaller gifts such as disks, CDs, gift certificates, and jewelry so you're not stuck carrying around large packages. Also, have the presents wrapped right in the store. Paying an extra dollar will save you the headache of wrapping at home.

If you're a stickler for doing things yourself, decorative bags are an easy (and attractive) way of wrapping gifts. Gift bags can be expensive, but many discount retailers and dollar stores offer inexpensive lines of gift bags, tissue paper, and accessories. Keep all the bags you receive so that you can reuse them.

Invariably, there's someone you'll forget to shop for until the last minute. When this happens, go with the trusty gift certificate. Some malls offer mall-wide gift certificates that allow the recipient to choose a present at whichever store he or she prefers. Many people buy a few extra gifts in case they receive an unexpected gift from someone for whom they haven't purchased anything. Buying one or two extra gifts is fine, but any more than that is excessive.

If a friend has a special hobby, buy a gift certificate from the store that caters to this hobby. Keep in mind that some people feel more loved when thought is put toward their gift and consider gift certificates a quick fix. Others are ecstatic that they can get what they actually want. To make it easy on yourself, order as many gifts as you can online or through the mail. As long as you order products a few weeks before you need them, there should be no problem with them arriving on time.

Be careful when you order. Ask for a specific delivery date and call the day before to confirm the package was sent. Ensure that you know correct sizes before you order to avoid sending everything back next week.

While you're shopping for holiday gifts, pick up a few extra items for friends and family with birthdays only a month or two away. Although you may not want to think about another holiday, you won't have to go shopping a month after Christmas. Once you get all of your gifts home, keep all tags and receipts in one place where they are easy to find in case you need to take a gift back.

Most stores hold great sales on Christmas items a few days after the holiday. This is a good time to buy wrapping paper, greeting cards, bows, boxes, and the like. It's also an opportunity to stock up on holiday craft and art supplies. You'll have everything you need when you start on next year's ornaments, decorations, and lights for your house.

Organize Your Purchases and Related Paperwork

MUCH OF WHAT YOU BUY TODAY COMES WITH lengthy instruction manuals, warranty cards to be completed and mailed, and papers to file. How can you make optimal use of your purchases, master complex features, file the appropriate papers and packaging, and otherwise stay organized?

Prior to ever stepping foot in a store or ordering something online, determine in advance what you actually want the product to be able to do. If you wait until you are on the showroom floor to ascertain the functions and features that you want in an appliance or gadget, it will be too late!

Develop a checklist of associated benefits and features of products that are attractive to you. I use a purchasing checklist to help ensure that I am getting the best deal before I spend money on something. The following list discusses potential benefits and options related to stores or services responsible for selling the products you buy:

Discounts
- Are there quantity discounts or special terms?
- Are there corporate, government, association, or educator's discounts?
- Do they give weekly, monthly, or seasonal discounts?
- Do they offer frequent buyer discounts?
- Do they give off-peak discounts or odd-lot discounts?
- Do they offer a guaranteed lowest price?

Ordering Options
- Do they accept major credit cards?
- Do they accept orders by fax or by e-mail?
- Do they offer a money-back guarantee or other guarantee?
- Do they have a toll-free ordering line and a customer service line?
- Is it easy to reach a live operator?

Delivery
- Do they guarantee the shipping date? How do they ship?
- Do they offer free delivery and installation?
- Are their shipments insured?

- Are there shipping and handling charges?
- How long for delivery?
- What else is included?

Privacy
- At your request, will they keep your name off their mailing list?
- Do they intend to sell, rent, or transfer your purchase information to others?

Other Considerations
- How long have they been in business?
- Are authorized dealer/repair services in your area?
- Does the product come with a warranty?

Once on site, I am focused and ready with a single, slim piece of paper in my hand. Most consumers don't take any such steps to organize before a purchase because it seems like too much work. For me, it is less work to ensure that I acquire the right appliance, model, make, and capabilities than to discover too late that a purchase doesn't provide what I sought from the beginning.

When you're on site in a store, you want to give the appliance a good workout. With the salesperson, run through the steps that you would if you purchased the machine. Ensure that you understand how the darn thing works; don't wait until you're at home, on your own, and alone without guidance. Have the instructions explained to you repeatedly until you can't possibly fail.

The salesperson is there to serve you, the consumer, not the other way around. Arrive with the mindset that you are there to gather information, not necessarily to buy.

If you can't understand how to operate the unit and run through its basic functions while you are in the store, then perhaps the fault lies not with you, not with the salesperson, but with the manufacturer.

Think about clothes dryers, microwave units, blenders, combination radio and alarm clocks, and CD players and how some of them, mysteriously, seem to have instructions that are too ponderous to fathom, while others seem easy to operate.

Eschew thick instruction manuals. When contemplating an important appliance purchase, do you ask to see accompanying manuals? Some manufacturers think it is impressive to strap you with an 180-page instruction book.

As you peruse the packet of papers that comes with your appliance, including the instruction manual, diagram or schematic, and the warranty card, be on the lookout for the at-a-glance instructions. These are condensed onto a single page or card, often laminated, mercifully listing the 5, 8, 10, or 12 basic functions that 98 percent of buyers will use on a regular basis. If this card is illustrated or uses symbols or icons, all the better.

Taking the card in hand, see how easily you can operate the showroom model. Perhaps you need help from the salesperson at this juncture. That is okay; run through the card once with help, then a second time without it. If you can master what is on the card, then you've likely got it made in the shade.

Ideally, on the second run-through without help, you should be fairly adept at making the appliance operate as per the simple instructions. If not, maybe there is a make and model on the next shelf that is even easier to operate and still performs the basic functions that you're seeking.

To stay organized following the purchase of any appliances, equipment, or gadgets, file the receipt, diagrams, or schematics, and any other associated paperwork as you normally would with a purchase, but keep the instruction manual and the at-a-glance instructions near the appliance itself. This works particularly well for DVD and video players since, in many cases, you can simply place the instructions under the unit.

Recognize that fewer switches, buttons, or dials may not mean that a product is less sophisticated or offers fewer benefits or features. Indeed, the opposite may be true. Only seek products and instructions designed with intelligence.

58

File Taxes on Time and Without Grief

KEEPING ACCURATE, COMPLETE TAX INFORMATION is a fundamental component in the life of the organized individual or family. You don't have to be concerned about the IRS at any time if you take simple steps to ensure that you have the documentation necessary to back up your tax returns.

Any office supply store today sells a variety of notebooks, binders, folders, dividers, and other office supplies that enable you to quickly and easily house the various documents, receipts, and vouchers related to both your income and your expenses. Some people maintain all of their deductible tax receipts in a folder with a compartment for each month of the year. Other, more involved folders allow you to file receipts on a weekly basis over the course of 52 weeks.

Personally, I find that a three-ring binder works as well as anything. You can insert dividers for each month, and add three-hole punched plastic sleeves that enable you to both store and view the receipts and documentation you accumulate. If your expenditures in any given month are considerable, simply use more than one sheet for that month.

If you own property, you can make room within your binder specifically to record and house transactions related to such ownership. The same is true for other types of tax-related issues, such as expenditures for childcare, employee business expenses, job search information, and depreciable assets.

A decent guide for how to set up your tax binder often comes from reviewing tax returns from previous years. Notice what kinds of forms you filed. You'll likely need room in your binder for that particular tax-related concern for the coming year as well. Some people use financial management software to record all income and expenses immediately after every transaction throughout the year. This is fine if you can maintain that kind of diligence. I've found that it is unnecessary to use such programs to stay organized and effectively complete your taxes on time.

For most people, the majority of expenditures can readily be traced through the family checkbook and major credit cards. Increasingly, the major vendors, especially Visa and MasterCard, issue a convenient, concise compendium by category of all expenditures you have made in the past year.

Obviously, if you make any cash expenditures that may be tax-deductible, you need to get a receipt. This could include cash donations to charitable organizations or any other out-of-pocket disbursements. To keep things easy for yourself, establish the practice of paying by credit card or check for everything that remotely could be deductible on your tax return. That way, you will have complete documentation at the end of the year between these two major sources of financial information.

Pick a day and take the receipts and documents and begin allocating them into like areas such as "airfare," "hotels," "work supplies," "school supplies," "utility bills," and "auto maintenance and repair." You already know these categories as you have been dealing with them for years!

You may end up with 15 or 20 piles on the table before you. Completely allocate the entire stack until every single shred of paper is filed someplace. For those items that are difficult to classify, create a file called "miscellaneous." Then paperclip, staple, or fasten them together in some other way so that you have 15 or 20 reasonably neat piles.

Derive the sum for each category with a calculator, then write that sum on a sticky note attached to the first receipt. Then create a summary page of all the categories and all of the totals.

Carefully review your itemized statement from your major credit card company to include any expenses that showed up on their concise roster that weren't otherwise in your year-long file folder. Afterward, do the same with your checkbook.

If you wrote a check for an item that is deductible, but you have no other documentation for it, add that sum to the appropriate category. When you're done, you will have all the expense information you need to successfully make complete and accurate claims on your tax returns, or at least enough documentation to survive an audit without too much damage.

About Your Income

Proceed in the same way with wage or earning statements. Continue categorizing, fastening, and summing until you produce a single sheet which encapsulates your yearly income. This provides you with a clear, complete documentation with which to file your taxes.

If you have received any notices from the IRS or your state's department of taxation in previous years, reread the notices, especially if they involved a correction to your statement. In that way, you can minimize the chance of making the same error for the current year's statement.

Tax Preparation Software

Tax preparation software is perfected! If you are already using it, then you know how much faster and easier it is to prepare your taxes

than it was in the days when you had to tediously proceed line by
line through each of the tax forms you were obligated to file. If you
haven't used tax preparation software before, start now or face
another 15 hours of complete and utter drudgery.

There are two major vendors of tax preparation software:
Kiplinger's Tax Cut and Quicken's Turbo Tax. Such software can save
you hours of time and frustration when completing your tax returns.
The variation among software programs is not prodigious. Each program has a user-friendly interface. You start off listing basic information, then simply hit a button that says "next." As you answer one
question after another, the software assembles your information for
appropriate and highly accurate use throughout your tax returns.

Based on the answers to the questions you provide, you proceed
down one trail or another. The software is designed so that you automatically file the forms that you need to complete based on your tax
situation. Each of the software programs contains options that allow
you to return to a prior screen, change data or information, prepare a
tax worksheet on the fly, or examine actual return information.

Tax preparation software also allows you to pose "what if" questions. In other words, if you elect to file one way versus another, you
can quickly see the ramifications of your selection.

Handling State Income Taxes

In nearly every state in the union you also have to file state income
taxes. These forms are somewhat less rigorous than IRS paperwork.
Completing your state income taxes takes but a fraction of the time
that is required to file your federal income taxes. Again, use your
returns from prior years to serve as reasonable guides as to how to
complete your current year's state return.

How does one get started on state taxes? I suggest buying the
state versions of tax preparation software. Many of the vendors will
give you a discount off the state version if you have already bought

their federal version. When you use state tax preparation software, your overall transaction time is greatly reduced, often to 10 minutes or less. You have the satisfaction of knowing that there is a decent probability that the forms have been filled out correctly. Your printer spits them out in rapid fashion, and as with the federal forms, they come to you neat, complete, and ready to be mailed.

If you send in your returns before March 15th, you are reasonably assured of receiving a refund before next year. After April 1st, you are competing with the masses who have procrastinated. As April 15th approaches, you are one of many taxpayers nationwide who are racing to get their forms turned in on time.

This may seem funny in a book on organization, but seek to help the IRS as much as you can. It's only really one person at the IRS who reviews your tax returns. Any explanations you can offer above and beyond the minuscule amount of space provided on the form can prove to be quite helpful. Moreover, it shows the IRS agent that you are a conscientious citizen and taxpayer, and that you are trying to be helpful. This can only work in your favor.

List the phone numbers where you can be reached and even your e-mail address. Any agent can find this information about you with ease, so you might as well provide it up front.

After you've sent in your tax return, what better time to relax?

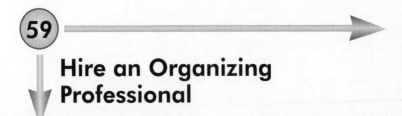

59

Hire an Organizing Professional

GOT HELP? HAVE YOU EVER CONSIDERED THE SERVICES of a professional organizer? They can be of significant assistance. Professional organizers will charge you at least $60 per hour. The good ones help you to not only get organized, but to stay organized as well. Together, you examine the areas of your life that have become disorganized and rearrange them so that they work for you.

A good professional organizer stresses principles not merely placement. If you have an organizer arrive and simply "do everything for you" without teaching principles and without making you take an active role in the process, you're not likely to maintain any of your places and spaces. Sure enough, in a matter of time, things will become disorganized again.

When you know the reason for putting pens to the right, paper in the top center drawer, and so on, you have a better chance of maintaining your system. After the professional organizer departs, do you want to be a long-term dependent? I mean, come on, do you want to have to pay somebody a pretty penny or voluminous stacks of $20 bills every time your stuff gets out of control? I think not!

If you think it makes sense to have a professional organizer help you for some finite number of sessions, or on a regular basis, then your best bet is to contact the National Association of Professional Organizers (NAPO):

> *National Association of Professional Organizers*
> *35 Technology Parkway South, Suite 150*
> *Norcross, Georgia 30092 USA*
> *770-325-3440 Fax: 770-263-8825*
> *e-mail: hq@napo.net*

Like any well established professional association, NAPO maintains an active Web site, *www.napo.net* to help you identify members in your local area. If you read and actually follow the tips in this book, however, you'll have no need to pay good money for a professional organizer.

60

Divide, Literally, and Conquer

WHEN I WAS 14 YEARS OLD, my mother suggested that I reorganize our utility closet. Even at that tender age, I realized that this tiny little room would never stay organized unless I had some way to divide and permanently separate items. The room was about five-by-five feet with no door; it simply had an entranceway downstairs next to the laundry room. As you entered, to the right there were five built-in shelves; to the left there were a couple of clothing hooks hung in a single row for coats and jackets.

Although it was a small room, it was a mess beyond reason and hope. The room served as our household catchall and contained tennis balls, wires, excess telephone cords, gloves, mittens, nuts and bolts, flashlights, batteries, and some objects whose identity I couldn't figure out for the life of me!

I hunted throughout the house to find empty shoeboxes and was able to gather about six or seven, which seemed like enough. I returned to the utility closet and began grouping like items together. I started with the middle shelf because it was the easiest to see and reach. There were enough stray tennis balls, racket balls, Ping-Pong balls, and golf balls to fit in one large shoebox. Then I used another shoebox to house wires, phone cords, extensions, extra light switches, wall outlets, and other small electrical stuff.

Since I didn't have all the shoeboxes I needed, I placed mittens, gloves, and scarves neatly in between the "ball" box and the "electrical" box. Using another shoebox, I housed extra door stoppers, furniture savers (small, circular rubber mats that go under table legs and couches to preserve the rugs), dusting items, a whisk broom, and other stuff that didn't seem to fit anyplace else.

In the next space, I assembled cans and canisters that would remain upright and in place, such as insect spray, three-in-one oil, poison ivy lotion, plant food sprayers, and other such items. Once again, I did not use a shoebox; instead, I let the borders between shoeboxes serve as a compartment. Now the entire shelf, which consisted of five compartments, was complete. The shelf was visually pleasing and much more organized than before I had started. I went on to tackle the other shelves in the same manner and spirit.

In the space between the floor and the bottom of the first shelf, I placed the largest items—those, which, if they were to fall, would cause a ruckus. On higher shelves, I placed the lightest items, those seldom used, and perhaps most importantly, those that could easily be seen by a shorter person such as my mother.

Some of the items I encountered didn't belong in this utility closet at all. No surprise about that. I relocated such items to their proper homes in the garage, the laundry room, the kitchen, or the back deck. Some items didn't merit retention, so I went ahead and threw them away. Some items were unnecessary duplicates, so I gave them away.

When the project was complete, I stood back and examined the results. The closet that had been a total mess was now neat, functional, and (dare I say it?) roomy! The actual time to rearrange each shelf was no more than a few minutes. Reallocating items that were best suited in other locations throughout the house took several more minutes, but this was not a difficult task.

A few years later when I was a senior in high school and then a college student, my organizational efforts in this particular room continued to prevail—no lie! Literally dividing up the items and creating permanent separations was the key. Sure, a couple of items were out of place, and the compartments on each shelf weren't quite so neat.

Also, some new items had been put in the closet (presumably for me to come by and integrate!). Still, six years after my initial efforts, even in the face of the entropy that predictably transpires in a household of six people, the utility closet essentially remained organized. My organizational artistry had prevailed.

The insights I gained from this task stayed with me over the following decades: If you have the right containers, dividers, and tools at your disposal, the physical organization of a space or place in your life is entirely manageable. You can win. You can keep your possessions in order. You can find them when you need them. You can then show off your marvelous work.

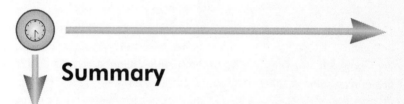

Summary

WITH EACH PASSING YEAR, and more specifically, each day, hour, minute, and second, an increasing amount of information is generated on earth and an accelerating number of technological breakthroughs are achieved. Therefore, maintaining organization in your career and personal life will only grow in importance.

Fortunately, you have the skills, the smarts, and the fortitude to stay in control. Even if you have a highly demanding job and considerable professional and personal responsibilities, you can succeed magnificently. When you acknowledge that you steer the rudder, flip the switch, pull the lever, call the shots, and have the power within you to take steps to make your life more organized, a wondrous result occurs—your life starts to become more organized. If you've resolved to get organized in your life, then you're well on the road to this achievement. Nothing can stop you.

Bibliography

Archibald, Russell. *Managing High-Technology Programs and Projects.* New York: Wiley, 1998.

Aslett, Don. *Clutter Free Finally and Forever.* Pocatello, ID: Marsh Creek Press, 1995.

Cathcart, Jim. *The Acorn Principle.* New York: St. Martin's Press, 1998.

Davidson, Jeff. *101 Internet Marketing Secrets.* Irvine, CA: Entrepreneur Press, 2002.

Davidson, Jeff. *Breathing Space.* New York: MasterMedia, 2000.

Davidson, Jeff. *The Complete Guide to Public Speaking.* New York: Wiley, 2003.

Davidson, Jeff. *The Complete Idiot's Guide to Managing Stress.* New York: Alpha Books, 2001.

Davidson, Jeff. *The Complete Idiot's Guide to Managing Your Time.* New York: Alpha Books, 2002.

Davidson, Jeff. *The Complete Idiot's Guide to Reinventing Yourself.* New York: Alpha Books, 2001.

Davidson, Jeff. *Marketing Yourself and Your Career.* Avon, MA: Adams Media, 1999.

Davidson, Jeff. *The 60 Second Procrastinator.* Avon, MA: Adams Media, 2003.

Felton, Sandra. *Messie's Manual.* Grand Rapids, MI: Fleming Revel, 1983.

Fritz, Robert. *Path of Least Resistance.* New York: Ballantine, 1989.

Hall, Edward. *The Hidden Dimension.* New York: Doubleday, 1966.

Hedrick, Lucy. *Five Days to an Organized Life.* New York: Bantam Doubleday Dell, 1990.

Hemphill, Barbara. *Taming the Paper Tiger.* Washington: Kiplinger Books, 1996.

Kimeldorf, Martin. *Serious Play, A Leisure Wellness Guidebook.* Berkeley: Ten Speed, 1994.

Kostner, Ph.D., Jaclyn. *Knights for the TeleRound Table.* New York: Warner, 1994.

Levasseur, Robert. *Breakthrough Business Meetings.* Avon, MA: Adams Media, 1994.

Markham, Ursula. *The Elements of Visualization.* Rockport, MA: Element Books, 1989.

Maslow, Ph.D., Abraham. *Toward a Psychology of Being.* New York: Wiley, 1968.

Moore-Ede, Ph.D., Martin. *The Twenty-Four Hour Society*. Reading, MA: Addison-Wesley, 1993.

Moskowitz, Robert. *How to Organize Your Work and Your Life*. San Diego: Mainstream Books, 1981.

Oliver, Joan Duncan. *Contemplative Living*. New York: Dell Books, 2000.

Pagonis, William. *Moving Mountains*. Cambridge, MA: Harvard Business School Press, 1992.

Salsbury, Glenna. *The Art of the Fresh Start*. Deerfield Beach, FL: Health Communications, 1995.

Sugarman, Joe. *Success Forces*. Chicago: Contemporary Books, 1980.

Williams, Paul. *Getting a Project Done on Time*. New York: AMACOM, 1996.

Wydra, Nancilee. *Designing Your Happiness*. Torrance, CA: Heian International, 1995.

Wydra, Nancilee. *Feng Shui Goes to the Office*. New York: Contemporary Books, 2000.

Zeer, Darin. *Office Yoga: Simple Stretches for Busy People*. San Francisco: Chronicle Books, 2000.

About the Author

JEFF DAVIDSON KNOWS A THING OR TWO about getting organized, and how to enhance one's professional and personal life as a result. Some people think of Jeff as a dynamo who has wracked up an impressive list of accomplishments. Still, he finds time to travel the world, stay in shape, spend time with his daughter, and keenly pursue a wide variety of intellectual interests. More importantly to you, Jeff is among the best at offering solutions to the time pressures and life balance problems that people face today—people like you! Jeff mixes "tried and true" advice with fresh insights and innovative solutions to the daily career and personal problems that often confront people.

Jeff has been featured in 68 of the top 75 newspapers in America, based on circulation, including *USA Today, The Washington Post, The Los Angeles Times,* and the *Chicago Tribune.* As a five-time state winner of the United States Small Business Administration's Media Advocate of the Year Award, Jeff has published more than 3,300 articles on the topics of entrepreneurship, management and marketing effectiveness, and life balance in nearly every type of magazine, journal, newsletter, and web 'zine.

Jeff's speeches have been featured in *Vital Speeches of the Day* on six occasions along with those of Dr. Henry Kissinger, Lee Iacocca, George Bush (senior), William Bennett, Michael Eisner, Jimmy Carter, Alan Greenspan, and the Dalai Lama. He has shared the spotlight on covers of magazines with Tony Robbins and with Dr. Wayne Dyer.

For six years running, Jeff has averaged 100,000 books sold annually in the highly competitive fields of self-help, business, and how-to books. Some of his titles include *The 60 Second Procrastinator, The Complete Guide to Public Speaking, Breathing Space,* and *The Complete Idiot's Guide to Time Management,* along with five other titles in that series.

As a professional speaker, Jeff has attracted clients such as American Express, America Online, IBM, Wells Fargo, NationsBank, Swisshotel, Westinghouse, and more than 700 other leading organizations and associations including the U.S. Treasury, National Association of Realtors, Club Managers Association of America, and the American Congress of Healthcare Executives.

Jeff can be found on the web at *www.BreathingSpace.com* and reached via e-mail at *KeyNoteSpeaker@BreathingSpace.com.* He resides in Chapel Hill, North Carolina.